yellow earth

**Yellow Earth Theatre and Royal Exchange Theatre
in association with Black Theatre Live present**

Mountains:
The Dreams of Lily Kwok

by In-Sook Chappell
Adapted from *Sweet Mandarin* by Helen Tse

The first performance of *Mountains: The Dreams of Lily Kwok*
was at the Royal Exchange Theatre on 22 March 2018

CAST

Siu-See Hung	Helen
Tina Chiang	Lily
Matthew Leonhart	Leung, Kwok Chan
Andy Kettu	Hideki, Japanese Soldier
Minhee Yeo	Kit Ye, Tai Po, Mrs Lee
Ruth Gibson	Mrs Woodman, Miss Price, Hostess
Rina Takasaki	Gong, Waitress, Mabel

CREATIVES AND PRODUCTION

In-Sook Chappell	Writer
Jennifer Tang	Director
Amelia Jane Hankin	Designer
Amy Mae	Lighting Designer
Elena Peña	Sound Designer
Ruth Chan	Composer
Lucy Cullingford	Movement Director
Jerry Knight-Smith CDG	Casting Director
Chris Frith	Tour Production Manager
Chris Radford	Company Stage Manager
Isabel Llinos Sullivan	Assistant Stage Manager

Thanks to Lan Kwan (Cantonese Translations)

Sweet Mandarin by Helen Tse is published by Random House

Mountains: The Dreams of Lily Kwok was jointly commissioned by the Royal Exchange Theatre and Yellow Earth Theatre

UK Tour sponsored by the **Hong Kong Economic and Trade Office, London (HKETO).**

 John Ellerman Foundation

CAST

SIU-SEE HUNG (Helen)

Theatre credits include: *O Deptford* (Albany Theatre); *Much Ado About Nothing*, (Polka Theatre); *Chinglish* (Park Theatre); *LSO Discovery: Play on Shakespeare* (Barbican Theatre); *A Colder Water Than Here* (Vault Festival); *The Blue Bird* (Wimbledon Studio/Albany/Putney Arts Theatre); *Diaochan – The Rise of the Concubine* (Arts Theatre/ Red Dragonfly Productions); *The H-Word* (RIFT/New Diorama); *I Wish To Die Singing* (Finborough Theatre); *A First Class Death* (Vault Festival); *A Dream From a Bombshell* (Trikhon Theatre & The Albany); *Velocity* (Finborough Theatre); *Obamamerica* (Theatre 503); *Granny Dumpling, Ba Banh It* (Yellow Earth and Albany); *Big Fridge* (Hen & Chickens Theatre); *Thief, Dim Sum Nights* (Yellow Earth Theatre); *Our Town* (King's Head Theatre) and *Something There That's Missing* (Edinburgh Festival).

Film credits include: *Jade Dragon, Adult Content, Receptionist, Unexpected ReunionN, Upstage, Sketchpack, The Fighting Room* and *Terminal.*

TINA CHIANG (Lily)

Tina studied at RADA and is making her first appearance for the Royal Exchange Theatre.

Other theatre credits include: *Labour of Love* (Headlong/Michael Grandage Company); *Chimerica* (Headlong/Sonia Friedman Productions); *Cyrano De Bergerac* (Southwark Playhouse); *Still Ill* (Kandinsky/Shuffle *Festival*); *From Shore To Shore* (Freedom Studios); *M.Butterfly* (GBS, RADA); *Fox Attack* (National Theatre of Scotland/Oram Mor); *Hong Kong Impressions* (CAS/Theatre Noir); *Why The Lion Danced* (Yellow Earth Theatre/UK Tour); *From Bangkok To Burnley* (National Theatre Studio); *Wave/Boom* (Yellow Earth Theatre/UK Tour) and *Girls' Night* (Royal Court YPT).

TV credits include: *Bodyguard, Rellik, Kiss Me First, Fearless, Coronation Street, Emmerdale, Casualty, Doctors, All About The McKenzies, Billionaire Boy, Tyrant* and *Run.*

Radio credits include: *Inspector Chen Mysteries, The Last Of The Pearl Fishers* and *The Birthday Gift.*

MATTHEW LEONHART (Leung, Kwok Chan)

Matthew is making his first appearance for the Royal Exchange Theatre.

Other theatre credits include: *Project New Earth* (China Arts Space); *The Last Days Of Limehouse, Dim Sum Nights* (Yellow Earth Theatre); *From Shore To Shore* (Freedom Studios); *The Stars That Play With Laughing Sam's Dice* (Pentameters Theatre); *The Sugar-Coated Bullets Of The Bourgeoisie* (Finborough Theatre); *B.O.B The Final Cut* (Hong Kong Architecture is Art Festival); *L'Orphelin (The Orphan of Zhao)* (Taiwan Frank Festival); *The Lost Dreamachine* (WOT Productions); *Sandman* (Frenzy Productions); *Invisible Glass* and *Peach Blossom Fan* (Redcat, Los Angeles).

Television credits include: *Berlin Station* (season regular); *50 Ways To Kill Your Lover, Treasures Discovered, New Worlds* and *Channel V Countdown*.

Film credits include: *Philophobia, The Accidental Spy* and *Too Loud A Solitude.*

ANDY KETTU (Hideki, Japanese Soldier)

Andy recently graduated from the Royal Conservatoire of Scotland and is making his professional debut for the Royal Exchange Theatre.

Credits in training include: *Romeo and Juliet; The Burial At Thebes; The Snow Queen* and *Table*, which played at the Citizens Theatre.

Film credits include: *Carapace.*

He also performed in *Dream On!*, which live streamed on BBC Arts as part of the Shakespeare 400 celebrations.

MINHEE YEO (Kit Ye, Tai Po, Mrs Lee)

Minhee trained at The Poor School, University of Oxford and is making her first appearance for the Royal Exchange Theatre.

Other theatre credits include: *Just One More Time* (The Space, One Festival); *One Day, Maybe* (dreamthinkspeak, Hull UK City of Culture 2017)); *Chinglish* (Park Theatre); *Replay* (C Venue, Edinburgh Festival) and *Leodo: The Paradise* (Maro, Edinburgh Festival).

Television credits include: *Strike Back: Legacy, Cuffs* and *Wasteman.*

Film credits include: *Avengers: Age of Ultron, Kotchebi* and *A Perfect Turn.*

RUTH GIBSON (Mrs Woodman, Miss Price, Hostess)

Theatre credits include: *1984* (Live Reading, The Orwell Foundation); *Blackout* (Harlow Playhouse); *The Patriotic Traitor, The Dead Monkey* (Park Theatre); *The Story Project/ The Circle* (Arcola Theatre); *Theatre Uncut* (Soho Theatre); *You Once Said Yes* (Winner of a Fringe First and Total Theatre Award, Look Left Look Right); *Intimate Exchanges* (Mercury Theatre, Colchester); *O Brave New World* (Retz); *The Hit* (Two Shoes and Cake); *The Kitchen* (National Theatre); *Portmanteau* (Arcola Theatre); *My Wonderful Day* (Stephen Joseph Theatre/New York/National Tour); *Man Of The Moment, Private Fears In Public Places* (Royal & Derngate); *Independent Means* (winner of a MEN Award for Best Actress in a Leading Role); *Vieux Carre* (Manchester Library Theatre); *Life and Beth* (Stephen Joseph Theatre/National tour); *Snake In The Grass, Touch Wood, Forget Me Not Jane* (Stephen Joseph Theatre); *The Bear* (Traverse/National Tour); *Anne Of Green Gables* (Sadler's Wells); *Markings* (Southwark Playhouse/UK Tour); *After Mrs Rochester* (winner of an Evening Standard Award for Best Play, Duke of York Theatre); *Blood Brothers* (Phoenix Theatre); *Dawn (Rei-Mei)* (Etcetera Theatre/Japan Tour).

Television credits include: *The Pact, The Littlest Boho, Babylon, The Culture Show, Doctors* and *Judge John Deed*.

Film credits include: *Moomins On the Riviera, Christmas Tree, Good Girl-Bad Girl, The Fridge* and *Capital*.

RINA TAKASAKI (Gong, Waitress, Mabel)

Rina trained at The Urdang Academy and is making her first appearance for the Royal Exchange Theatre.

Other theatre credits include: *Avenue Q* (UK Tour).

Television credits include: *Breaking The Band* and GMTV.

Film credits include: *The Forest, Level Up, Wrong Direction, Meanwhile* and *Tomoko*.

Rina has appeared in various adverts and music videos, most recently played the featured role in Mc Fioti's *Bum Bum Tam Tam*.

CREATIVES

IN-SOOK CHAPPELL (Writer)

In-Sook was born in South Korea but raised in England. She studied dance in New York at the Alvin Ailey School before moving into acting. She started writing in-between acting jobs. Her first play *This Isn't Romance* was produced at the Soho Theatre after winning the Verity Bargate Award and was commissioned as a screenplay by Film4 with In-Sook as writer/director. It was also broadcast on BBC Radio 3 and enjoyed a sell-out Korean production at the National Theatre Company of Korea this summer.

Theatre credits include: *Tales of the Harrow Road* (Soho Theatre); *Absence* (Young Vic Theatre) and *P'yongyang* (Finborough Theatre). *The Free9*, her Connections play for the National Theatre, is in the 2018 canon and being produced around the country.

She is currently on attachment at the National Theatre Studio. In-Sook has also made two short films as writer/director, *Full* and *Kotchebi*.

JENNIFER TANG (Director)

Jennifer trained at the University of East Anglia, the Young Vic and on the National Theatre Studio Director's course. She was resident assistant director of Theatre Royal Plymouth/The Drum 2013-14.

As director: *We Are You You* (Young Vic, British Museum) *Clytemnestra* (The Gate, London); *WANTED* (West Yorkshire Playhouse); *Constellations* & *One Day When We Were Young* (GEST, Sweden); *Listening to Hackney* (Chatsworth Palace); *For The Record* (TRP, Plymouth); *The Hour We Knew Nothing Of Each Other* (The Drum, Plymouth); *Blow Out; Feathers; The Forum* (Etcetera Theatre, London and Bike Shed Theatre, Exeter); *Chasing Beckett* (The London Theatre).

In development: *Gwei Mui* (Ghost Girl); *Fundamental.*

As assistant/associate: *Imperium Parts I and II, Snow in Midsummer* (RSC); *Weaklings* (National Tour); *The Edge of Our Bodies* (Gate Theatre); *Madman; Solid Air; Inside Wagner's Head* (The Drum, Plymouth); *#Aiwewei* (Hampstead Theatre); *The Magic Flute* (Ryedale Festival & Arcola Theatre) *The Owl and the Pussycat* (Royal Opera House, London); *Rodelinda* (Iford Arts).

AMELIA JANE HANKIN (Designer)

Amelia trained at RADA and the RSC.

Upcoming design credits include: *Europe After The Rain* (Mercury Theatre).

Recent design credits include: *Fog Everywhere* (Camden People's Theatre); *Mixed Brain* (Tiata Fahodzi and Summerhall, Edinburgh); *The Scar Test* (Soho Theatre); *Punts* (Theatre503); *Natives* (Southwark Playhouse); *Powerplay* (Hampton Court Palace); *Good Dog* (Watford Palace Theatre); *The Same Deep Water As Me* (Guildhall); *Rudolf* (West Yorkshire Playhouse); *The Crucible* (Guildhall); *Torch* (Edinburgh Festival); *We Are You* (Young Vic); *Bricks and Pieces* (RADA/Latitude); *The Neighbourhood Project* (Bush Theatre); *This Is Art* (Shakespeare in Shoreditch); *The Tiger's Bones* (Polka and West Yorkshire Playhouse); *The Little Prince* (Arcola); *Pinter Triple Bill* and *Dealer's Choice* (Guildhall); *Night Before Christmas* (West Yorkshire Playhouse,) *She Called Me Mother* (Black Theatre Live, Pitch Lake Productions and National Tour); *Fake It 'Til You Make It* with Bryony Kimmings and Tim Grayburn (National Tour, Traverse Theatre and Soho Theatre) and *64 Squares With Rhum and Clay* (National Tour and Edinburgh Festival).

Amelia's designs for The Itinerant Music Hall were exhibited at the V&A Museum as part of the *Make/Believe UK Design for Performance* exhibition July – January 2016.

AMY MAE (Lighting Designer)

Amy works across Theatre, Dance, Site Specific and Devised performance. Amy designed the lighting for the acclaimed 'Pie Shop' version of *Sweeney Todd: The Demon Barber Of Fleet Street*, which is currently playing at the Barrow Street Theatre in New York. She won the Knight of Illumination Award in 2016 for the London production, and her designs for the New York production have been nominated for the 2017 Drama Desk Award for Outstanding Lighting Design and the Lucille Lortel Award for Best Lighting.

Upcoming credits include: *Br'er Cotton* (Theatre503) and *Exploding Circus* (Pavilion Theatre, Worthing).

Recent credits include: *Othello*, *Jekyll And Hyde* and *The Host* (Nyt Rep Season 2017); *Half Breed* (Talawa – Soho Theatre & Assembly Rooms); *Start Swimming* (Young Vic/Summerhall Edinburgh); *The Ugly One* (Park Theatre); *Babette's Feast* (The Print Room); *The Lounge* (Soho Theatre); *Wordsworth* (Theatre by The Lake); *Paradise Of The Assassins* (Tara Theatre); *Knife Edge* (Pond Restaurant, Dalston); *Minaturists 55* (Arcola Theatre); *Prize Fights* (Royal Academy of Dramatic Art); *Orphans* (Southwark Playhouse); *Macbeth* (Italia Conti); *I'm Not Here Right Now* (Paines Plough Roundabout and Soho Theatre); *Liola* (New Diorama Theatre); *Children In Uniform*; *Punk Rock* (Tristan Bates Theatre); *Sweeney Todd* (Harringtons Pie and Mash Shop, and West End); *The Three Sisters* (Cockpit Theatre); *Cat Couture* (Music Video); *In Bed* (London Theatre Workshop); *Henry V* (Royal Academy of Dramatic Art); *Pool*, *The Gut Girls* (Brockley Jack Theatre) and *The Legacy* (The Place).

ELENA PEÑA (Sound Designer)

Current and forthcoming productions include: *Misty* (Bush Theatre) and *All Of Me* (China Plate).

Theatre credits include: *The Caretaker* (Bristol Old Vic & Northampton Royal and Derngate); *Thebes Land* (Arcola); *Hir* (Bush Theatre); *Years Of Sunlight* (Theatre 503); *The Bear/The Proposal* (Young Vic); *Sleepless* (Shoreditch Town Hall, Analogue Theatre, Staatstheater Mainz); *The Christians*, *I Call My Brothers*, *The Iphigenia Quartet* (Gate Theatre); *Patrias* (Sadlers Wells Theatre, Paco Peña Flamenco Company, Eif); *Ant Street*, *Brimstone And Treacle*, *Knives In Hens* (Arcola Theatre); *Islands* (Summer Hall, Edinburgh, Bush Theatre & Tour); *Brainstorm* (National Theatre & Park Theatre); *The Kilburn Passion*, *Arabian Nights* (Tricycle Theatre); *Macbeth* (Hightide, Wac & Tour); *Not Now Bernard* (Unicorn Theatre); *Pim* & *Theo* (Odsherred Teater, Denmark, Nie); *Flashes* (Young Vic).

Sound installation credits include: *Have Your Circumstances Changed?* and *Yes These Eyes Are The Windows* (Artangel).

Television/online credits include: *Brainstorm* Live at Television Centre (BBC4 and iPlayer).

Radio credits include: *Duchamps Urinal* (Recordist/Sd/Editor, BBC Radio 4); *The Meet Cute* (Recordist/Sd/Editor/Musician, BBC Radio 4); *Twelve Years* (Recordist/Sd/Editor, BBC Radio 4).

Elena is an Associate Artist for Inspector Sands where her credits include: *The Lounge* (Soho Theatre – Offie Nomination for Best Sound Design).

RUTH CHAN (Composer)

Ruth is a renowned composer for film, television and theatre. Her soundtrack for silent film *Around China With A Movie Camera* (British Film Institute) has been performed at Flatpack Film Festival and China Changing Festival at Royal Festival Hall. She has also composed for television documentaries including *A Very British Airline*, (BBC); *Attack of the Pentagon* (Discovery Channel) and *The Trouble With Pirates* (BBC).

Theatre credits include: *Snow In Midsummer* (Royal Shakespeare Company – nominated for The Stage Debut Award for Best Music); *Shangri-La* (Finborough Theatre); *The Last Days Of Limehouse* (Yellow Earth Theatre) and double bill *Magical Chairs* and *There's Only One Wayne Lee* (Southwark Playhouse & Beijing International Fringe Festival).

Other credits include: *The Triumph of Time* for clarinet trio and actor (Thailand International Composition Festival, Pianoforte Studio Chicago, Shakespearean Theatre Conference Stratford, Ontario); *From the Top* (Hong Kong Arts Festival); *Turandot Reimagined* (Tête-à-Tête Festival) and *Piccadilly Revisited* (China Arts Space, Royal Opera House Linbury studio, Hong Kong Arts Festival, UK Now Festival Beijing).

LUCY CULLINGFORD (Movement Director)

Lucy has an MA in Movement Studies from The Royal Central School of Speech and Drama.

Lucy collaborates regularly with the RSC and recent productions as movement director include: *Coriolanus*, *Snow In Midsummer; The Tempest; Don Quixote* and *The Jew Of Malta*.

As movement practitioner in the Movement Department at the RSC productions include: David Farr's *The Winter's Tale*, Greg Doran's *Hamlet*, *Love's Labour's Lost* and *A Midsummer Night's Dream* (Courtyard Theatre).

As movement director recent work includes: *The Winter's Tale* (National Theatre & tour); *The Shadow Factory* (Nuffield Theatres); *The 101 Dalmatians* (Birmingham Rep); *King Lear* (Chichester Festival Theatre); *Jenufa* (Grange Park Opera); *East Is East* (Northern Stage and Nottingham Playhouse); *Abigail's Party* (Theatre Royal Bath); *The Wakefield Mystery Plays*, (Wakefield); *Of Mice and Men* (Birmingham Rep); *My Mother Said I Never Should*, (St James's Theatre); *The Night Before Christmas*, (West Yorkshire Playhouse); *Talking Heads*, (Theatre Royal Bath); *Constellations* (Trafalgar Studios, UK National Tour, Manhattan Theatre Club, Broadway, Duke of York's Theatre and Royal Court). Lucy was the RSC/Warwick University Creative Fellow in Residence where she directed *The Renaissance Body*. The piece was staged to mark the re-opening of the Swan Theatre, Stratford and performed at the University of Warwick and as a live installation at the British Museum as part of the *Shakespeare: Staging The World* exhibition for the World Shakespeare Festival in 2012.

As choreographer productions include: *The Last Mermaid* with Charlotte Church, (Wales Millennium Centre); *Alice in Wonderland* (CBBC) and *The Secret Adversary* (Watermill Theatre).

BLACK THEATRE LIVE

Black Theatre Live is a pioneering national consortium of eight regional theatres led by Tara Arts, committed to effecting change nationally for Black, Asian and Minority Ethnic touring theatre through a sustainable programme of national touring, structural support and audience development.

Black Theatre Live is a partnership of Tara Arts (London); Derby Theatre, Queen's Hall Arts (Hexham); Lighthouse (Poole); Theatre Royal Bury St. Edmunds, Theatre Royal Margate, Stratford Circus Arts Centre (London) and Key Theatre (Peterborough).

Black Theatre Live launched in 2015 and has toured Tara Arts' *Macbeth* directed by Jatinder Verma; *She Called Me Mother* with Golden Globe and BAFTA nominee Cathy Tyson; award-winning *The Diary of a Hounslow Girl* by Ambreen Razia; the UK's first all-black *Hamlet* directed by Jeffery Kissoon; *An Evening With An Immigrant* with Inua Ellams and Fuel prior to his season at the National Theatre; and in autumn 2017 we toured *Big Foot* by Joseph Barnes-Philips with HighRise Theatre.

In 2018 we pilot an Associate Artist tour with Lighthouse, Poole and Phoebe McIntosh of *Dominoes;* and co-production with Yellow Earth Theatre and Royal Exchange, Manchester of *Mountains: The Dream of Lily Kwok* by In-Sook Chappell.

Black Theatre Live is supported by Arts Council England, Esmee Fairbairn Foundation, John Ellerman Foundation and Ernest Cook Trust.

Find out more at **www.blacktheatrelive.co.uk** **@BlackTLive**

Tara Arts for Black Theatre Live

Jatinder Verma	Artistic Director
Jonathan Kennedy	Associate Producer
Laurie Miller-Zutshi	Executive Director
Claudia Mayer	Associate Director (Design)
Alexandra Wyatt	General Manager
Jyoti Upadhyay	Marketing & Communications Manager
Katie Robson	Digital Communications Coordinator
Andy Grange	Technical & Operations Manager
Ian Parlane	Head of Finance at FE Solutions
Xiao Hong (Sharon) Zhang	Finance Office

ROYAL EXCHANGE THEATRE

Manchester's Royal Exchange Theatre Company transforms the way people see theatre, each other and the world around them.

Their historic building, once the world's biggest cotton exchange, was taken over by artists in 1976. Today it is an award-winning cultural charity that produces new theatre in the round, in communities, on the road and online.

The Exchange's unique auditorium is powerfully democratic, a space where audiences and performers meet as equals, entering and exiting through the same doors. It is the inspiration for all they do; inviting everyone to understand the past, engage in today's big questions, collectively imagine a better future and lose themselves in the moment of a great night out.

The Royal Exchange has just been awarded School of the Year at *The Stage* Awards 2018. The Spring–Summer Season features work from an incredible array of artists from across Manchester and beyond. It includes new adaptations of Mary Shelley's FRANKENSTEIN by April De Angelis; a new play by Associate Artist Maxine Peake, QUEENS OF THE COAL AGE, alongside her return to the stage to play Winnie in Samuel Beckett's HAPPY DAYS. Associate Artists RashDash and new partners Yellow Earth bring their distinctive performance styles to The Studio.

Find out more at **www.royalexchange.co.uk** **@rxtheatre**

Registered Charity Number 255424

NATIONAL TOUR 2018

Thurs 22 March - Sat 7 April
ROYAL EXCHANGE THEATRE
St Ann's Square, Manchester, M2 7DH
Box Office: 0161 8339833

Wed 18 to Sat 21 April
STRATFORD CIRCUS ARTS CENTRE
Theatre Square, Stratford, London, E15 1BX
Box Office: 020 8279 1080

Tues 24 to Wed 25 April
THEATRE ROYAL BURY ST EDMUNDS
Westgate Street, Bury St Edmunds, Suffolk, IP33 1QR
Box Office: 01284 769505

Fri 27 to Sat 28 April
LIGHTHOUSE
21 Kingland Road, Poole, Dorset, BH15 1UG
Box Office: 01202 280 000

Tues 1 to Wed 2 May
KEY THEATRE
Embankment Road, Peterborough, PE1 1EF
Box Office: 01733 207 239

Sat 5 May
THEATRE ROYAL MARGATE
Addington Street, Margate, CT9 1PW
Box Office: 01843 292 795

Thurs 10 to Sat 12 May
DERBY THEATRE
15 Theatre Walk, St Peter's Quarter, Derby, DE1 2NF
Box Office: 01332 59 39 39

Wed 16 to Sat 19 May
WATFORD PALACE THEATRE
20 Clarendon Road, Watford, WD17 1JZ
Box Office: 01923 225 671

Mon 21 to Wed 23 May
SHEFFIELD CRUCIBLE THEATRE
55 Norfolk Street, Sheffield, S1 1DA
Box Office: 0114 249 6000

Thurs 24 to Fri 25 May
QUEEN'S HALL ARTS CENTRE
Beaumont Street, Hexham, Northumberland, NE46 3LS
Box Office: 01434 652 477

Wed 30 May to Sat 2 June
BELGRADE THEATRE
Belgrade Square, Coventry, CV1 1GS
Box Office: 024 7655 3055

In-Sook Chappell

Mountains:
The Dreams of Lily Kwok

Adapted from *Sweet Mandarin* by Helen Tse

OBERON BOOKS
LONDON

WWW.OBERONBOOKS.COM

First published in 2018 by Oberon Books Ltd
521 Caledonian Road, London N7 9RH
Tel: +44 (0) 20 7607 3637 / Fax: +44 (0) 20 7607 3629
e-mail: info@oberonbooks.com
www.oberonbooks.com

A catalogue record for this book is available from the British
Library.

PB ISBN: 9781786824875
E ISBN: 9781786824882

Cover image: Jon Shard

Printed and bound by 4edge Limited, Essex, UK.
eBook conversion by CPI Group (UK) Ltd, Croydon, CR0 4YY.

Visit www.oberonbooks.com to read more about all our books and to buy them. You
will also find features, author interviews and news of any author events, and you can
sign up for e-newsletters so that you're always first to hear about our new releases.

Printed on FSC accredited paper

For my mothers & Audrey

Characters

Helen

Lily

Street Hawker

Leung

Hostess

Miss Price

Tai Po

Kwok Chan

Mrs Woodman

Waitress

Hideki

Japanese Soldier

Chinese Prisoner

Kit Ye

Gong

Mrs Lee

Mahjong Players

Mabel

The play can be performed by a cast of seven actors.

Setting

Hong Kong and At Sea. In the present and the past.

HONG KONG

1.

The sound of an aeroplane. A shadow passes the stage.

The tone before an announcement.

CAPTAIN'S VOICE: Ladies and Gentlemen, we've just been cleared to land at Hong Kong International Airport and are starting our descent.

FLIGHT ATTENDANT'S VOICE: *(In Cantonese.)* Ladies and Gentlemen, the Captain has advised that we've started our descent to Hong Kong International Airport. Please make sure your seat backs and tray tables are securely fastened in the full upright position... *(The voice fades out.)*

HELEN walks down a staircase, she's tired but excited. She wears a simple dress, ballet shoes. People move past her on the staircase, mostly Chinese with one Westerner. HELEN reaches into her bag and takes out her passport. Two lines form: Chinese and foreigners, HELEN hesitates, then takes her place behind the other Westerner.

The sound of a high-speed bullet train.

The two lines are thrown forward at speed and with force.

HELEN is deposited into the mad swirl of Hong Kong.

Music and the cacophony of Hong Kong: snatches of Cantonese, building work, traffic, the distinctive Hong Kong pedestrian signal.

A movement sequence. Hong Kong never stops. Work hard, play hard, constant action. HELEN walks quickly with purpose, searching, she changes direction, moves fast. The crowds close in on HELEN, she hesitates, doesn't know which direction to turn, feels like she can't breathe, panics.

HELEN cries out. The crowds disperse leaving her alone onstage. Frantically she scans the faces in the audience, doesn't recognise anyone.

LILY'S VOICE: How are you?

HELEN stands still, tired, overwhelmed. She shakes her head.

HELEN: Still jetlagged, I haven't slept in days, drunk far too much black coffee.

Pause.

HELEN: I've never felt so British.

Sound of LILY laughing. HELEN smiles.

HELEN: My Cantonese is terrible and my Mandarin is even worse. I thought that here I'd blend in but I'm enormous, I'm the English girl who grew up in a chippy. The Hong Kong girls are tiny and immaculate wear heels and twinsets in this heat… I've never felt as lost as I do here. This morning I tried taking a shortcut, got stuck in a shopping mall, kept going round in circles, interconnected never-ending shopping malls, the same shops in different places: Gap, Zara, Mango, J Crew, Starbucks… It's not what I…

A STREET HAWKER enters on another part of the stage pushing a metal trolley, stops and starts to cook on the hot plate.

HELEN: It's too busy here, all I do is work and …rush. There are too many people but nobody who matters and I'm always on my own. I miss you and Manchester, miss your cooking. I tried… but cooking for one's depressing.

The smell of cooking fills the theatre. HELEN inhales, walks towards the STREET HAWKER.

HELEN: *(In Cantonese.)* Give me one portion.

The STREET HAWKER doesn't understand.

HELEN: *(In English.)* One portion please.

The STREET HAWKER hands HELEN a portion of siu mai.

HELEN: Siu mai. The smell reminds me of you, of home.

HELEN eats.

LILY appears.

HELEN closes her eyes.

HELEN: I haven't slept. I'm seeing things. It's normal. Don't panic.

HELEN takes a deep breath, opens her eyes.

HELEN: You're still here.

LILY: So I am. I thought you might not recognise me.

HELEN: Popo, I'd know you anywhere. You look the same but... young.

LILY: I never stopped feeling like this... inside.

HELEN: Am I dreaming?

LILY: Maybe. In my dreams... I'm always this age.

HELEN reaches out to touch her, tentatively at first then holds her tight.

HELEN: You're really here.

LILY: Yes.

Pause.

HELEN: How long's it been?

LILY: Over forty years.

LILY looks over at the metal trolley.

LILY: There are still dai pai dongs.

HELEN: Yes.

LILY looks around her.

HELEN: Do you recognise it?

LILY shakes her head.

LILY: Where are we?

HELEN: Central.

LILY: Where are the Colonial shanty town buildings?

HELEN: They don't exist anymore.

LILY looks up.

LILY: All skyscrapers now.

HELEN: I'm constantly going up and down in lifts. Look, my office is in there, the house of a thousand arseholes.

LILY: Because of the round windows?

HELEN: Yes and full of bankers and lawyers.

LILY nods proudly.

LILY: You're one of them.

HELEN: Yes.

HELEN offers LILY a siu mai.

HELEN: Wait.

HELEN goes over to the metal trolley, takes a bottle of soy sauce and adds a dash, then gives it to LILY.

LILY eats the siu mai.

LEUNG enters pushing a wooden cart loaded with barrels. He is thin and dressed in rags. LILY can see him but HELEN can't. He walks over to the STREET HAWKER, sets down his cart, looks at the siu mai.

LEUNG: Those would taste even better with Leung's soy sauce.

STREET HAWKER: I have soy sauce.

LEUNG: But not mine. Mine's …special, will give you the edge over your competition.

LEUNG pours soy sauce into a glass, swirls it around.

LEUNG: It's Chinese, grown and made in Guangzhou.

LEUNG smells the soy sauce as if it were a fine wine.

LEUNG: Hmm… malty and sweet.

He holds it up to the nose of the STREET HAWKER who nods.

LEUNG: We mix the beans with special seeds and roasted wheat. That's what gives it the richness and depth.

LEUNG dips a chopstick into the soy sauce.

LEUNG: Here, this is the true test.

The STREET HAWKER opens his mouth and LEUNG places a drop of soy sauce on his tongue.

STREET HAWKER: Not bad.

LEUNG gives him a look.

STREET HAWKER: Pretty good.

LEUNG: I sell direct to you.

STREET HAWKER: No merchants?

LEUNG: Correct.

The STREET HAWKER whistles.

LEUNG: You get a great product at a good price and my men get fair wages /for their work.

The STREET HAWKER shakes his head, exits.

HELEN: /Just like you make them.

LILY: What?

HELEN: The siu mai.

LILY: Oh yes… When we first came to Hong Kong I used to go with my father to sell his soy sauce. I was seven years old… sometimes I'd be given siu mai. To me… the taste was… heaven.

HELEN: It still is.

LILY looks at HELEN, at her well-cut dress, expensive shoes and handbag.

LILY: In those days we lived on a daily bowl of rice and soy sauce. We went without, dreamed of…

LEUNG: Once upon a time… there was …a man who had his own ideas about things.

LILY: *(Softly.)* Like you.

LEUNG: One day this man announced to his village that he was going to build a road south to the Han River. The problem was there were two mountains that stood in the way. The villagers laughed and mocked him said…

LEUNG acts out an ignorant villager.

LEUNG: 'How stupid you are. How can one old man move two entire mountains?'

LILY smiles.

LEUNG: The old man replied, 'though I shall die, I shall leave behind my son and my sons son. Since the mountains cannot grow taller I see no reason why we won't be able to level them.' After five generations the mountains were levelled and the road built.

LILY: What if there aren't any sons?

LEUNG looks at LILY.

LEUNG: The daughters take the place of the sons.

Pause.

LEUNG: Even though you're a girl you'll earn a place for yourself in the world through hard work. Do you want to improve the lives of your children and grandchildren?

LILY: Yes.

HELEN looks at LILY, can't see LEUNG and he can't see her.

HELEN: You dreamed of… a better life?

LEUNG exits.

LILY: Why else would a person leave their home? What they know? Why did you?

HELEN: Opportunity, adventure, more money and less tax. This is China.

LILY: Yes. This is China now.

HELEN: China's exciting, full of possibilities. The world's changed.

LILY looks around her.

LILY: Yes.

HELEN: Everyone wants a piece of China. Anyone with any sense wants to trade with China, wants Chinese investment. Chinese money is regenerating Manchester, could regenerate the whole of the North of England.

HELEN looks at LILY.

HELEN: Aren't you proud?

LILY: Because China's rich now?

HELEN: Yes. I used to be …ashamed, used to sleep with a clothes peg on my nose.

LILY looks at HELEN.

LILY: I love your nose.

HELEN: We have the same nose.

LILY: The same face. Your mother looks nothing… somehow you came out like me.

HELEN: Yes, but the English version.

LILY: Do you ever think about what it cost?… The success you so admire.

They look at each other.

HELEN: It wasn't just money that brought me here. I thought I might find... I thought Hong Kong might be home but it's not... I look Chinese but I'm not...

LILY: You are.

HELEN: No. I'm a fake. I don't belong here.

LILY: Don't say that. You have Chinese blood.

Pause.

HELEN: The family story I was told starts in a chip shop in Middleton. Look at me, us. That can't be where my story starts. Why don't you ever talk about your life before?

LILY: Silence... is a tradition.

HELEN: Bullshit. Why haven't you told me about Hong Kong?

LILY: Because you don't talk about...

HELEN: About what?

LILY: Tragedies... Don't question... You have to move on, push forwards, upwards.

HELEN: No. I'm... There's a gap... I can't explain, I'm not... there's something missing. That's why I came to Hong Kong.

LILY looks at HELEN.

LILY: Memories can be unsettling, painful things...

HELEN: Please.

LILY looks around.

LILY: That building...

HELEN: Popo, it's the Mandarin Oriental.

LILY: No, that's not it. I've been there. It's... It used to be the Queens Building. I worked downstairs in the kitchens.

HELEN: Let's go inside.

2.

Early evening. A stylish bar: floor to ceiling windows, Hong Kong stretches out all lit up.

The HOSTESS repositions a minimal flower arrangement and incense sticks. She is Caucasian but dressed in heels and a cheongsam.

HOSTESS: *(In Mandarin.)* Good evening.

LILY: *(In English, slightly hesitant.)* A table for two?

HOSTESS: *(In English with an Australian accent.)* Are you guests of the hotel?

HELEN: No. Is that a problem?

HOSTESS: Not at all madam.

HELEN: We'd like to sit by the window.

LILY picks up a couple of sticks of incense.

LILY: Could I?

HOSTESS: No worries, follow me.

The HOSTESS leads them to a table by the window.

HELEN: Two glasses of champagne.

The HOSTESS nods, walks away. HELEN and LILY look out of the window.

LILY: So many lights.

HELEN: There's Wan Chai… There's the harbour.

LILY looks at the harbour.

LILY: My first view of Hong Kong was from the Guangzhou ferry pulling into the harbour. I was a country girl, all our possessions in one large bundle. I had never seen so many buildings packed close together, so many people… On the docks I saw my first white man, I thought he was a giant.

The HOSTESS brings two glasses of champagne.

HELEN: Thank you.

The HOSTESS walks away. HELEN lifts her champagne glass.

HELEN: To grandmothers and granddaughters, even though we look like sisters. Gonbei.

LILY: To you. My Granddaughter. Everything was worth it. Yamsing.

They drink champagne.

HELEN: When did you work here?

LILY: ...I was twelve years old. Just before I was taken on by an amah agency.

HELEN: ...I didn't know you were an amah.

LILY: It was my very first ambition.

HELEN: To be a maid?

LILY looks at her.

LILY: I was a poor Chinese girl from the slums.

Pause.

LILY: The first time I climbed up to the peak, I would have been ...eight? The air's different up there. Clean, smells like... jasmine. I walked along Robinson Road, it was another world... grand white houses... I'd never seen such green grass and flowers planted everywhere. I thought the white women were like magical beings. I saw a Chinese girl, a couple of years older than me. She wore a black silk dress, was holding a white baby. That was what I wanted. To look after a white baby, to work at a big house on the peak.

HELEN looks at LILY.

LILY: My father was ambitious, wasn't content to stay an impoverished peasant in Guangzhou. He wanted more than the village. In Hong Kong I wanted more than the slums...

I knew I had to keep taking steps towards… I started to attend the Union Church on Kennedy Road.

HELEN: But you're Buddhist.

LILY: I knew I had to learn English and it was the only place a girl like me could be taught for free. I said what they wanted to hear but inside I was Buddhist.

LILY lights a stick of incense and places it in a small vase on the table.

LILY: I was me.

MISS PRICE enters, she wears a severe dress from a bygone era, her hair scraped back.

MISS PRICE: *(Calling out.)* Lily Leung.

HELEN glances at LILY.

MISS PRICE: *(Impatiently.)* LILY LEUNG.

LILY: You go. You're the one that's curious about my past. I've already been there.

HELEN walks over to MISS PRICE who hands her a uniform without looking at her.

MISS PRICE: Now put that on.

MISS PRICE pointedly turns her back on HELEN. HELEN puts on the white tunic and black trousers. MISS PRICE turns around, scrutinises her.

MISS PRICE: You look the part. We're looking for new girls to take on as junior amahs.

HELEN looks at MISS PRICE and grins.

HELEN: Great.

LILY: STOP!

MISS PRICE and HELEN freeze.

LILY: Don't look at her and don't talk unless what she says demands a reply. You're a poor Chinese girl, you have to understand about class.

HELEN: Popo, I grew up in Britain.

LILY: There are the economic and Confucian class divides and then there's Colonial rule... Westerners first, Chinese second. Keep your eyes down.

HELEN looks at LILY, then she looks down at the floor. MISS PRICE walks around her.

MISS PRICE: You look the part. We're looking for new girls to take on as junior amahs.

HELEN looks down at the floor.

MISS PRICE: For every ten girls I interview I'll only take on one, possibly two. Now, why should you be one of the lucky ones?

HELEN lifts her eyes. MISS PRICE is looking at her.

MISS PRICE: Don't tell me a sob story. I only hire discreet professionals.

HELEN: I'm very very hard working and if you were to give me this opportunity I won't let you down.

MISS PRICE: You all say that.

HELEN looks down at the floor.

MISS PRICE: We are the premier agency on the Island. We supply staff of distinction. Now you have one last chance to tell me why I should hire you, what makes you a cut above the other girls?

HELEN looks at LILY.

HELEN: ... As well as speaking English I've taught myself to read and write a little.

MISS PRICE: In English?

HELEN: Yes M'am, and basic arithmetic.

MISS PRICE: You're educated.

HELEN: I… No… I attended classes at the…

HELEN looks at LILY.

LILY: Union Church.

HELEN: Union Church.

MISS PRICE: You're Catholic?

Pause, before HELEN nods.

MISS PRICE: That does set you apart from the other Chinese girls.

MISS PRICE looks at HELEN with approval.

MISS PRICE: We insist that our girls follow the three P's. Promptness, politeness and polish. There are no set holidays or rest days but some employers allow a half day of rest every fortnight. You'll probably want to go to Church.

HELEN nods enthusiastically.

MISS PRICE: If you are one second late or fall short of your employers' satisfaction by a fraction you will be dismissed instantly. You'll be blacklisted and never get another amah position. Do you understand?

HELEN: Yes m'am. Does that mean?

MISS PRICE hands HELEN a document to sign. HELEN starts to read it.

LILY: Just sign it.

HELEN: *(Quietly to LILY.)* These are terrible terms.

LILY: There's no negotiation here. If I don't become an amah, I won't get the opportunity to go to England and if I had stayed I don't believe you'd be a lawyer, you might not even exist.

HELEN signs the document, hands it back to MISS PRICE.

MISS PRICE: You will attend two weeks of training. The cost will be deducted from your wages.

HELEN nods in agreement.

LILY: I was taught how to shine intricate pieces of silverware. Learned how to sweep, wash and then polish a floor.

MISS PRICE: Catch.

MISS PRICE throws a sheet at HELEN. LILY and HELEN throw the sheet up into the air, it billows.

LILY: I learned to make a bed with sheets, Irish linen, Chinese wasn't good enough.

MISS PRICE: A good amah is never idle. She works from six in the morning until after her employers have gone to bed.

LILY: She cleans the house from top to bottom every day.

MISS PRICE: She cooks delicious meals, bakes cakes for afternoon tea.

LILY: Looks after and loves the children too.

MISS PRICE exits with the sheet.

LILY: Becoming an amah was my first opportunity. I saw it for what it was. I didn't hesitate. I grabbed it. I had… responsibilities.

HELEN: At twelve?

LILY: It wasn't my first job.

Steam fills the theatre.

LILY: I went to work in a silk factory when I was five.

The sound of metal cogs whirring around the auditorium.

LILY: I worked seven days a week, twelve hour shifts, had to stand all the time in the heat with the steam and deafening noise.

HELEN looks at her.

LILY: My family needed my wages to make the next step. My father wasn't going to sell his soybeans, he was going to make his own soy sauce and that takes time. Every minute I was terrified.

HELEN: How did you bear it?

The steam and noise ease off.

LILY: I imagined myself wearing a brand new silk jacket. When I was tired and hungry and my whole body ached I imagined sitting down to a feast with my father and mother and...

TAI PO and LEUNG appear at a low table laden with food and a present tied with a bow. They are well dressed in new clothes.

HELEN: And?

LILY: It came true.

LEUNG opens the present. TAI PO takes out a child's red silk jacket. (The jacket signifies LILY as a child.)

LILY: On my twelfth birthday I wore a new red silk jacket, sat at a table laden with more food than we could eat.

TAI PO and LEUNG eat.

LILY: My father was a successful man. He had built his business in seven years. His soy sauce sold as fast as he could make it. It was Leung's soy sauce you'd find in the kitchens of the new Peninsula Hotel.

HELEN: Wow...

LILY: We had moved out of the slums and into a new flat with a view of the harbour.

LEUNG stands up.

TAI PO: Where are you going?

LEUNG: Upriver.

TAI PO: To the factory?

LEUNG nods.

TAI PO: I made red bean buns.

LEUNG: Save me one, no two.

TAI PO: *(To LILY as a child.)* Tell him to stay. It's your birthday. If you beg him he'll stay.

Pause.

VOICE OF LILY CHILD: Joy geen. See you tomorrow.

LEUNG smiles at LILY as a child and walks out. LILY watches him.

LILY: That was the last time I saw him.

HELEN: …How come?

LILY: He …died.

HELEN: I'm… sorry.

LILY: I was a girl. The business, the property, the money couldn't be passed on to… A nephew inherited everything. He cut us off.

TAI PO weeps, her body wracked with grief. Savagely she turns on LILY as a child.

TAI PO: Why didn't you beg him to stay?

TAI PO packs the red silk jacket back into the box.

LILY: That was the end of my childhood.

LILY hands HELEN a stick of incense. HELEN lights it and places it in the small vase.

LILY is agitated.

LILY: Let's go to the harbour.

3.

Night. Victoria Harbour.

The sound of the sea.

LILY inhales and exhales deeply.

LILY: I love the smell of sea air can feel it stiff with salt.

HELEN: Popo, lighting the incense... I know it's something we do on special occasions but what does it mean?

LILY: I invited you into my past.

HELEN: Thank you.

LILY: And you invited me into your present. It links past present and future family.

    LILY walks away from HELEN.

LILY: I used to come here, look out at the boats setting off to the rest of the world.

    LEUNG appears carrying the birthday present.

LEUNG: Do you remember when we lived in Guangzhou and I told you about a magical place downriver called Hong Kong?

LILY: Yes.

LEUNG: Now Hong Kong is ordinary to us.

LILY: No. It'll never be ordinary to me.

LEUNG: It's home.

LILY: Yes.

LEUNG: There's another magical place.

LILY: What's it called?

LEUNG: The rest of the world.

    LEUNG and LILY look at each other.

LEUNG: I spoke to a sailor, he was born in Guangzhou, he's sailed all the way around the world. He's even been to England. He went somewhere called Liverpool and he told me there are Chinese people living there.

LILY: ...And wherever Chinese /people are they need Leung's soy sauce.

LEUNG: /people are they need Leung's soy sauce. Do you know what else my friend told me?

LILY shakes her head.

LEUNG: In Liverpool he saw a Chinese woman in a fur coat getting into a Rolls-Royce.

HELEN approaches. This time HELEN and LEUNG can see and hear each other.

HELEN: Popo.

LILY: This is Helen my granddaughter.

LEUNG looks at HELEN.

LEUNG: *(In Cantonese.)* You're an amah.

LILY: No. I was the amah, we were... nevermind. She grew up in England, Manchester, near Liverpool where your friend... She went to university, Cambridge.

LEUNG: *(In Cantonese.)* She's educated, went to school?

LILY: She's a lawyer. She's just as good as the white people. She can walk into places we would never dare, doors open...

LEUNG looks at HELEN, bows to her and HELEN bows back.

LEUNG: *(In Cantonese.)* You did it.

LILY: You always believed in me.

LILY holds onto LEUNG.

LILY: I wish… I wish I had held onto you like this. Hadn't let you go.

LILY looks at LEUNG's face.

LILY: If I had begged you to stay would you have?

Pause.

LEUNG: *(In Cantonese.)* You know better than to ever question the past.

LEUNG starts to walk away.

LILY: No. Baba, stay a while longer, please don't go.

LEUNG exits.

HELEN: It wasn't your fault.

LILY: Mother… Something in her broke, her mind wasn't… I had to look after her.

HELEN: Your responsibilities?

LILY: Yes. At first I lined up with the coolies for work by the hour. That's why becoming an amah… was the best, the pinnacle of what a girl like me could hope for.

A loud gunshot. HELEN and LILY jump in fright.

A shadowy male figure runs across another part of the stage.

HELEN: What's that in the water?

LILY: Where?

HELEN: There…

HELEN points at a shape in the water.

LILY: It's… No…

HELEN runs into the water.

LILY: Don't…

HELEN: It's… a body.

HELEN gives the body a tentative poke, then springs back. LILY turns away, breathes.

HELEN: It's a man… a boy.

HELEN pokes the body again, still no movement. Then she crouches down by his head.

HELEN: He's still breathing.

HELEN moves his hair off his face with a finger, looks at his face.

HELEN: Is this?

LILY: …Yes.

HELEN: You never talk about him… Neither does mum.

LILY: She didn't know him.

HELEN: When I was little I climbed up on a chair to look at his shrine on top of the tall cabinet. I saw his photo.

HELEN looks at him.

HELEN: He looks like mum.

LILY: Yes.

LILY looks at him.

HELEN: Tell me.

LILY: I was fifteen. The cook had sent me out…

KWOK CHAN sits up and coughs up sea water. HELEN leaps back in fright. CHAN doesn't see LILY, only notices HELEN, he smiles at her.

HELEN looks at LILY.

HELEN: *(To LILY.)* This is weird.

LILY: It's what you wanted. You're walking in my shoes. He thinks you're me. Never could see a woman over thirty.

HELEN turns back to CHAN.

HELEN: Are you alright?

CHAN looks down at himself and then at her, grins.

HELEN: Sorry, stupid question… What happened?

CHAN: I… think I might have fallen off a boat.

LILY: The water was rough this morning.

HELEN looks at him. CHAN looks at her smiles.

CHAN: I guess I'm lucky…

HELEN sees something in the water picks it up, it's a gun, shocked she throws it back in the water.

CHAN: It's not mine.

HELEN backs away.

CHAN: I promise I've never seen it before.

HELEN backs away. CHAN attempts to get up but he's still dizzy. HELEN moves towards him.

HELEN: Don't try to move yet.

Instinctively HELEN reaches out and touches his forehead, a moment of chemistry.

HELEN: You might be ill.

CHAN: Hmmm.

HELEN: You might have hypothermia.

CHAN: Maybe.

HELEN: Should see a doctor.

CHAN: Yes.

LILY: I offered to take him to the hospital.

CHAN checks in his pockets.

CHAN: It's all gone.

HELEN: What?

CHAN: My money.

They look at each other.

HELEN: We'll go to the police?

CHAN: No.

HELEN: People might be looking for you. Might be worried.

CHAN: I'm fine.

CHAN coughs.

HELEN: You're shivering, getting a fever.

CHAN: No. I've told you. I'm lucky. I'll be fine.

LILY: He was obviously ill. I thought I should take him home to mother, she'd know /what to do.

HELEN: /Come home with me.

CHAN looks at HELEN in amazement.

HELEN: I didn't mean it to come out like that.

CHAN: You don't look like the sort of girl to pick up strange men at the docks.

HELEN: I'm not.

CHAN grins at HELEN's embarrassment.

HELEN: I'm worried about you, that's all.

CHAN: Thank you.

HELEN: I found you, now I feel …responsible.

CHAN looks at her.

CHAN: You're pretty.

HELEN giggles nervously. CHAN struggles to his feet, bows to HELEN.

CHAN: Where can I find the ferry to Guangzhou?

HELEN: Are you from Guangzhou?

CHAN: Yes.

LILY: Keep going straight to pier 7.

HELEN: Pier 7.

CHAN bows to HELEN.

HELEN: Bai bai.

CHAN lurches off as if he's drunk, HELEN watches him.

HELEN: WAIT.

HELEN runs after him.

HELEN: Here take this.

She hands him some money.

HELEN: For the ferry.

CHAN looks at the money, it's a lot.

HELEN: The cook sent me out to buy fish, I buy direct from the fishermen, drive a hard bargain.

CHAN: …and do you cook?

HELEN: Yes.

HELEN glances at LILY.

HELEN: It's what I like to do best.

HELEN and CHAN look at each other.

HELEN: Say hello to Guangzhou for me.

CHAN: Do you know Guangzhou?

HELEN: I was born there.

CHAN: What's your name?

HELEN: Lily Leung.

CHAN: Lily Leung.

A moment before CHAN turns and walks away. LILY and HELEN watch him go. He turns and looks back at HELEN before he exits.

LILY glances at HELEN.

LILY: He had that effect on women.

HELEN: Is it disturbing that I feel …attraction for a man who looks like my mother… is in fact my grandfather?… I really need to sleep.

LILY: Not yet. There's work to do.

4.

HELEN stands in a large old fashioned kitchen peeling potatoes. MRS WOODMAN enters, she wears an elegant dress of draped silk, stands watching HELEN.

MRS WOODMAN: Do you like your work?

HELEN is startled.

HELEN: Yes m'am.

MRS WOODMAN paces.

MRS WOODMAN: Do you like coming up here every day?

HELEN: Yes m'am.

MRS WOODMAN: Why?

HELEN: I… I like to work. To be completely absorbed in what I'm doing, to do it well.

MRS WOODMAN: Interesting. Go on.

HELEN rapidly slices the potatoes into chips.

HELEN: I love to cook, to plan menus, adapt recipes, experiment. I love to shop for food, to choose the best vegetables, ripest fruits, freshest fish and quality meats.

Feeding people makes me happy… Up here… Everything sparkles… I can't imagine anything bad happening up here.

MRS WOODMAN laughs.

MRS WOODMAN: Gosh. That's certainly the most I've ever heard you say in one go.

HELEN: Sorry.

MRS WOODMAN: Why do you Chinese always look at the ground?

HELEN: We're told to m'am.

MRS WOODMAN: Look at me.

MRS WOODMAN stands like a statue. HELEN looks at her.

MRS WOODMAN: Well?

HELEN: …You're very beautiful.

MRS WOODMAN: What about this dress?

HELEN: It's …very beautiful.

MRS WOODMAN: It's from Paris. It's a Vionnet.

Pause.

MRS WOODMAN: I don't suppose you know what that is. If no one looks at you, you don't matter.

MRS WOODMAN sits languidly.

MRS WOODMAN: Sit down with me.

HELEN: Shall I bring you some tea?

MRS WOODMAN: No. Something… Is there wine left from luncheon?

HELEN: I'll check.

MRS WOODMAN: Don't bother I think it's… all gone.

MRS WOODMAN leans back.

MRS WOODMAN: If you were a man would you desire me?

An excruciating pause.

MRS WOODMAN: How old are you?

HELEN glances at LILY.

LILY: Fifteen.

HELEN: Fifteen.

MRS WOODMAN: Oh... It's hard to tell with you people.

HELEN: Mr Woodman's a very lucky man.

MRS WOODMAN: Yes he is.

HELEN: Will he be home for dinner?... I'm making his favourite.

MRS WOODMAN: Your guess is as good as mine. What do you think?

HELEN: ...He must work very hard.

MRS WOODMAN laughs.

MRS WOODMAN: He's decadent, likes to eat at the Pen. He likes ...China side.

MRS WOODMAN pats the chair next to her. HELEN sits down. MRS WOODMAN stares at her.

MRS WOODMAN: He has a mistress. China side.

HELEN's eyes widen.

MRS WOODMAN: I shouldn't tell you. You might get ideas.

MRS WOODMAN stares at HELEN's face.

MRS WOODMAN: It's hard with you people to know what you're thinking. Inscrutable... that's the word. I can understand it, wanting to taste the forbidden, the exotic. I'm adventurous too. You know a girlfriend and I went to a ...local restaurant, ate dimsum, we didn't know what we were ordering, some of it was quite nice. The point is it was different. An adventure. But then I came home.

MRS WOODMAN is crying.

MRS WOODMAN: Why is life so beastly?

HELEN looks at LILY who gives her a sharp look.

MRS WOODMAN: If this is all there is… what's the point? Sometimes… I can't bear it.

HELEN tries to comfort MRS WOODMAN.

MRS WOODMAN: I only really had one important choice to make in life. I made the wrong… Once you're married you're trapped.

LILY: We have a saying, 'having married a cock she must follow the cock. Having married a /dog she must follow…

HELEN: /'dog she must follow the dog. Having married a carrying pole she must carry it for life.'

MRS WOODMAN: It seems I've married a cock, not a terribly satisfying one so where's the benefit?

MRS WOODMAN stares at HELEN.

MRS WOODMAN: Maybe he's more satisfying to a Chinese girl… To a poor girl.

LILY brings over a box of bon-bons, hands them to HELEN who offers them to MRS WOODMAN.

MRS WOODMAN: I was beautiful. People were dazzled by me.

MRS WOODMAN eats bon-bons.

HELEN: You are beautiful. You are dazzling.

MRS WOODMAN offers HELEN a bon-bon.

LILY: *(To HELEN.)* You've never eaten chocolate before.

HELEN eats the bon-bon. MRS WOODMAN looks at her.

MRS WOODMAN: Hmmm I've introduced you to pleasure…
I had my pick. There was… He was handsome, he…
he made me nervous, occupied too much of my mind.

HELEN: Mr Woodman?

MRS WOODMAN: No not Mr Woodman. Not Mr Woodman
was a third son. Not marriage material. Unlike Mr
Woodman who I knew was wealthy. When he saw me his
eyes lit up. I may have mistaken admiration for love. I
married him because he didn't make me nervous. He wasn't
exciting. I thought he'd make a good husband, treasure me.

MRS WOODMAN eats bon-bons.

MRS WOODMAN: Marry the handsomest man you can. Marry
the one who drives you crazy. Because the dull, stodgy,
unimpressive ones are just as likely to be disappointing.

MRS WOODMAN exits with her bon-bons.

LILY: It turned out to be terrible advice.

HELEN: As if you'd ever take life guidance from a spoilt,
racist, self-pitying… You didn't did you?

LILY: I was fifteen, she made an impression. I thought she was
a woman of the world.

HELEN: The miniscule bubble at the very top of the peak.
'Why is life so beastly?' Bitch!

LILY: Helen!

HELEN: And you did marry the handsome man who drove
you crazy.

LILY: I did.

Pause.

HELEN: Come on… He's my grandfather, a quarter of me.
You have to tell me.

LILY: There wasn't much excitement in my life.

HELEN: It seems pretty dramatic to me.

LILY: You're getting one night of the edited highlights. Most of my life was work.

HELEN: Yep... I know that feeling.

LILY: Meeting Chan at the harbour... I thought about him. Made up stories in my head.

HELEN: That can be dangerous.

LILY looks at HELEN.

LILY: What aren't you telling me?

HELEN: ...I might be going on a date.

LILY: But you need to work. To focus. How many Chinese partners are there at your firm?

HELEN: None... I'm nearly thirty. I haven't felt... Popo, what if it never happens?

LILY: Perhaps it's better if it doesn't.

HELEN: No... I want... I work hard and take pride in my work. I earn good money. I can't complain but... there has to be something more.

Pause.

LILY: Who is he?

HELEN: He's called Hideki.

LILY: ...Japanese?

HELEN looks at LILY.

HELEN: Do you have a problem with me going on a date with a Japanese man?

5.

TAI PO enters carrying a green silk cheongsam, she looks at HELEN.

TAI PO: That won't do.

HELEN looks down at her amah uniform. TAI PO hands her the cheongsam.

TAI PO: Put this on.

HELEN holds it up.

TAI PO: Hurry up or we'll miss the celebrations.

LILY: They'll go on all night. It's liberation day. The war's over...

HELEN: War?

The sound of an explosion – fireworks.

HELEN: Where are we?

LILY: In Hong Kong.

HELEN: No. In the story.

The sound of cheering.

LILY: I'm about to meet Chan for the second time. I'm around your age.

HELEN: There was a gap that long?

LILY: Twelve years.

HELEN: We're jumping all over the place.

LILY: ...Memory comes the way it wants to. It's my story. I'll tell it my way.

TAI PO looks at HELEN, takes a red lipstick and puts it on her lips.

LILY: From the peak... I saw the Royal Navy sailing into the harbour.

The sound of shouting and laughter.

HELEN: It sounds wild out there.

TAI PO: I asked a friend to escort us.

HELEN: Who?

TAI PO: You don't know him. I met him at the hospital. The porter I was telling you about.

LILY: Mother...

HELEN looks at TAI PO.

TAI PO: You're over twenty-seven.

HELEN: Thank you. I know.

LILY: The war... wasn't conducive to... Too many young men died.

TAI PO: It's especially competitive now, you have to make even more of an effort.

HELEN: I...

CHAN enters. HELEN and CHAN look at each other, recognise each other.

TAI PO looks at HELEN, doesn't see CHAN.

TAI PO: You look lovely in that dress. With a little care and attention you could pass for ...twenty-three. Of course I'm worried people are starting to call you a left-over girl.

CHAN clears his throat, TAI PO turns.

TAI PO: Chan... meet my daughter Lily. Lily this is Kwok Chan.

CHAN grins at HELEN.

CHAN: Hello Lily Leung.

They look at each other.

HELEN turns to LILY, steps out of character.

HELEN: You recognised each other after all that time?

LILY: Yes.

HELEN: Nothing this romantic ever happens to me.

HELEN steps back into character.

Music plays.

CHAN: Do you dance?

CHAN starts to move to the music, grins at her.

CHAN: I think you want to.

HELEN: Yes, but I might not be very good.

CHAN: I think you'll be fine.

CHAN takes her by the arm and they start to dance. HELEN is stiff and awkward.

LILY and TAI PO stand watching them.

HELEN: Did you go back to Guangzhou?

CHAN: I walked to the pier, was about to buy my ticket and then... something told me to stay in Hong Kong, to try my luck.

HELEN looks up at him and smiles.

CHAN: It's hard to leave Hong Kong.

LILY: Yes but you made me.

CHAN: It's addictive.

HELEN: ...You might be right.

CHAN takes her by the hands and spins her around.

CHAN: Every time I go to the harbour I think about the pretty girl ...who wanted to take me home.

HELEN: I was worried about you.

CHAN: You aren't pretty anymore... You're beautiful. You've improved with time like all the best things.

They dance.

LILY: When men are this good with women they've usually had a lot of practice.

A table with a white tablecloth appears. CHAN leads HELEN to the table, pulls out her chair, they sit. TAI PO exits.

LILY: It was the first time I ever ate in a restaurant. When I was a child and went with my father to sell his soy sauce... I thought it must be the most wonderful, glamorous thing to eat in a restaurant. I'd stand and look in through the window at the elegant women in silk dresses and red lipstick...

A WAITRESS brings menus, recognises CHAN.

WAITRESS: I know you from Dragon. We don't want any trouble.

LILY: Signs I didn't pick up on.

CHAN: You're mistaken. We're here for dinner that's all. Bring us plum wine.

The WAITRESS nods, walks off.

LILY: I didn't want to see problems. I worked hard had lived through the war. I wanted to be happy, longed for...

LILY and HELEN's eyes catch.

LILY: I read through the entire menu, couldn't believe there was so much choice.

HELEN reads the menu, CHAN looks at her and smiles.

CHAN: What do you like to eat?

HELEN: Everything.

CHAN laughs.

CHAN: It's going to be an expensive evening.

The WAITRESS appears with two cups of plum wine.

39

CHAN: Order whatever you like.

HELEN: Thank you I will. *(To the waitress.)* Seaweed. *(To Chan.)* Do you like squid?

CHAN: I love squid.

HELEN: Salt and chilli squid.

CHAN: And soft shell crab.

HELEN looks at CHAN.

CHAN: If it's the first time… our first dinner together it has to be special. Do you want soup?

HELEN: Hot and sour.

CHAN: Make that two. Do you like char siu roast pork?

HELEN: Yes.

CHAN: It's my favourite.

They look at each other.

CHAN: Char siu roast pork belly, rice and choy sum.

The WAITRESS nods takes CHAN's menu.

HELEN: And mapo tofu… aubergines in chilli sauce and drunken chicken as well.

HELEN hands the WAITRESS her menu, grins.

CHAN: Quite an appetite you've got.

HELEN: I love eating.

CHAN laughs.

CHAN: Me too. I don't trust people who don't like to eat.

HELEN: No. You shouldn't.

CHAN looks at HELEN.

CHAN: Cooking is what you like best.

HELEN: Well remembered.

CHAN: What else?

HELEN: ...I love stories. Love to be told stories.

CHAN: Who tells you stories?

HELEN glances at LILY.

HELEN: My father used to.

CHAN: ...And now?

HELEN: No one.

CHAN looks at HELEN.

CHAN: That sadness in your eyes.

HELEN: Sorry.

CHAN: Don't be.

CHAN drinks.

LILY: STOP.

CHAN freezes.

LILY: Don't be desperate.

HELEN: I'm not.

LILY: It makes you ...vulnerable. Keep your eyes and ears open. See what's there not what you want to see.

HIDEKI enters, late twenties, glasses and a patterned sweater vest, so square he's almost cool, but not quite.

HELEN: Hideki.

HIDEKI walks towards HELEN, stops, checks his watch.

HIDEKI: *(Japanese/American accent.)* Exactly on time.

HELEN: Yes.

HIDEKI: I was worried I was late.

HIDEKI sits down. The WAITRESS walks over puts a drink down in front of HELEN.

HIDEKI: What are you drinking?

HELEN looks at the drink.

HELEN: A vodka martini.

HIDEKI: *(To the waitress.)* I'll have the same.

WAITRESS: How would you like it?

HIDEKI isn't sure, looks at HELEN.

HELEN: This is wet and dirty with an olive.

HIDEKI: *(To the waitress.)* I'll try that.

The WAITRESS nods, walks away.

HIDEKI: I like your dress.

HELEN: Thank you.

An awkward pause.

HIDEKI: Are you wearing it …ironically?

HELEN: …I just like it.

HIDEKI: Cool. Yeah so do I, it's very… *In the Mood For Love.*

HELEN: I'm nuts about that film.

HIDEKI: Right?

HELEN: That's what I thought Hong Kong would be like.

HIDEKI: A Wong Kar Wai movie?

HELEN: Dreamy and intense, insanely beautiful, atmospheric.

HELEN's rush of feeling is too much for HIDEKI who looks down at the table, picks up the drink and takes a gulp.

HELEN: That's mine.

HIDEKI: Oh… Sorry. I'm so sorry.

HELEN: It's not a big deal.

HIDEKI: I don't have herpes or anything.

An excruciating pause.

HELEN: It's good that you don't… I don't either.

HIDEKI stares down.

HELEN: You may as well….

HELEN pushes the drink towards him. HIDEKI takes a grateful gulp.

HELEN: Shall we start again?

HIDEKI: Yes please.

HELEN looks around.

HELEN: Do you come to Nobu a lot?

HIDEKI: Umm not really. All the traders say it's a good place to take a girl on a date if you want to… have a nice meal.

HELEN: Yeah… I've heard the food's good.

They look at each other, HELEN starts to giggle, it's infectious, HIDEKI starts laughing too.

HELEN: The good thing is this date probably won't get much worse.

HIDEKI: And that's good. How? If you want to leave, don't feel you have to stay to…

HELEN: I don't want to… leave. I've been looking forward to this evening.

HIDEKI looks at her.

HIDEKI: Really? I wanted to make a good impression. Aargh.

HIDEKI feels another wave of embarrassment.

43

HELEN: It's great that you're not …smooth, haven't had loads of practise.

HIDEKI: You've sussed that I'm a geek.

HELEN: I like geeks. I'm one too.

HIDEKI: You're a cute geek.

HELEN: We're fellow Asian nerds. Didn't have time for dating with Tiger parental pressure.

They laugh.

HELEN: How long have you been in Hong Kong?

HIDEKI: A year.

HELEN: How are you finding it?

HIDEKI: I work pretty hard. It can be lonely.

HELEN: Yes.

HIDEKI: It would be nice to find someone to spend time with.

A brief moment between them broken by the WAITRESS who sets down the second drink.

WAITRESS: Are you ready to order?

HIDEKI: We haven't even looked.

The WAITRESS walks away.

HELEN: Where did you grow up?

HIDEKI: Tokyo, but I studied in the US.

HELEN: MIT?

HIDEKI: Good guess.

HELEN: Maths PHD?

HIDEKI: …Or did you look me up on the company intranet?

HELEN: …How arrogant are you?

HIDEKI: Cambridge. First class honours. I looked you up.
I worked in New York.

HELEN: I know. Busted.

They grin at each other.

HELEN: We should look.

HIDEKI: Yeah…

HIDEKI picks up a menu.

HELEN: Do you like working in finance?

HIDEKI: I love it. It's just so exciting. I've always had a
thing about numbers. It's such a rush when I start to see
patterns emerging in the data, can piece together complex
algorithms.

HELEN: You're lucky. The luckiest people are the people
whose work is their passion.

HIDEKI: Working in finance isn't your passion?

HELEN: No.

HIDEKI looks at her in astonishment.

HIDEKI: You didn't always want to be a financial lawyer?

HELEN: …It was …expected that I'd go to university.

HIDEKI: Become a banker, lawyer, doctor?

HELEN: Yep. That's what my entire family was working
towards.

HIDEKI raises his glass.

HIDEKI: /Asian parents.

HELEN: /Asian parents.

HIDEKI: My mom would be so relieved if she knew I was on a
date with you.

HELEN: Really?

HIDEKI: She'd love you.

HELEN: She doesn't want you to marry a Japanese girl?

HIDEKI: Nah. She'd be thinking of the cute Asian babies.

HIDEKI looks down.

HELEN: We could be one of those Asian international finance couples that met in Hong Kong.

HIDEKI: When we get bored here we could do a stint in New York.

HELEN: I've never been.

HIDEKI: London.

HELEN: Been there done that.

HIDEKI: Tokyo.

HELEN: Is Japan still home for you?

LILY appears.

HIDEKI: Yeah. I think so.

LILY looks at HIDEKI with hatred.

HELEN: You still feel Japanese?

HIDEKI: Yes.

HIDEKI can sense LILY.

HIDEKI: Excuse me. I just need to… That drink went straight through me.

HIDEKI gets up and exits quickly.

HELEN: The war was a long time ago.

LILY: It feels… no… the past, it's all around us.

CHAN stirs.

CHAN: Who tells you stories?

HELEN is startled.

CHAN: That sadness in your eyes... Can I tell you a story?

HELEN: Yes.

CHAN: Once upon a time there was a poor farmer from Guangzhou.

HELEN drinks plum wine.

CHAN: He wasn't like the other peasants, dared to want more for himself and his family. He decided not to sell his soy beans but to make it into soy sauce himself. He took a gamble, sold it downriver in Hong Kong.

HELEN glances at LILY, drinks plum wine.

CHAN: It paid off and soon the farmer was a wealthy man.

LILY: Seven years of trudging the streets.

CHAN: His factory in Guangzhou thrived, he took on more men, paid them fair wages. He inspired the other peasants to want more. But he'd made a dangerous enemy.

HELEN: ...A merchant?

CHAN: A rival manufacturer. Wong.

HELEN drinks plum wine.

CHAN: Wong's family had been trading for five generations.

HELEN: Who cares? I have more respect for a man who's born with nothing and through guts and hard work makes his own success.

CHAN: Me too.

They look at each other.

CHAN: But Wong didn't think that way. He wanted to buy your father's business at a fraction of its value. Your father refused.

HELEN: He was looking out to the rest of the world.

CHAN: Wong threatened him. Your father was brave, refused to be bullied.

HELEN: Go on.

CHAN: Wong paid a thief to set the factory on fire. Your father walked in and disturbed him. The thief panicked, struck him with an iron bar.

HELEN: ...He was murdered?

CHAN: Yes.

HELEN steps out of character, turns on LILY in anger.

HELEN: Why haven't you told me?

Pause.

HELEN: What else are you keeping from me?

LILY: So now you know that my father who I loved more than anyone was murdered. How do you feel?

Pause.

LILY: How do you think I felt?... That's how I found out. You wanted to walk in my shoes, well that's what you're doing. I didn't get forewarnings, wasn't prepared for...

HELEN steps back into character and faces CHAN.

HELEN: He didn't suffer?

CHAN: No. He died quickly.

LILY: If only...

HELEN glances at LILY, understands.

HELEN: ...I had begged him to stay.

CHAN looks at her.

CHAN: It wasn't your fault.

LILY breathes.

LILY: I suspected my father was murdered but it was a mystery that Chan solved.

HELEN: It wasn't your… my fault.

CHAN: You were a child, how could it have been.

LILY nods, breathes.

HELEN: *(To Chan.)* How do you know all this?

CHAN: After that first meeting…

HELEN: At the harbour.

CHAN: I tried to forget you but your serious expression kept popping back into my head.

HELEN: I thought about you too.

CHAN: I asked around about Lily Leung.

HELEN: Who did you ask?

CHAN: …Old friends from Guangzhou.

HELEN glances at LILY.

HELEN: Triads?

CHAN: …Yes.

Pause.

CHAN: Your father sounds like an incredible man.

HELEN: He was.

CHAN: I… want to be honest with you.

HELEN looks at him.

CHAN: I've spent some time in the wrong company...
But that's in the past. I've changed. I want... to deserve you.

HELEN and CHAN look at each other.

HELEN: The way you look at me.

CHAN: Should I stop?

HELEN: No. Don't stop.

CHAN reaches for her hand.

CHAN: Strong people find a way to be happy.

HELEN nods.

CHAN: We need to search out a lot of joy to balance such sad
memories... Could we be happy together?

HELEN: ...Yes.

CHAN: I see you and you're ...extraordinary. Something,
someone special.

They look at each other.

HIDEKI enters. CHAN freezes.

HIDEKI: It's so awkward when they have the attendant in the
bathroom. I mean how much do you tip?

HELEN: Err...

HIDEKI sits down.

HIDEKI: I mean how much is it worth? They squeeze soap
onto your hand and then hand you a towel. Ten Hong
Kong? Twenty?

HELEN: ...I don't think you should have to pay to go to the
loo.

HIDEKI: Loo, that's cute. See, that's another thing we have in
common.

He smiles at her.

HIDEKI: But then if you don't tip you feel like a real cheap bastard.

LILY: Does he know his history?

HELEN: I'm sure…

HIDEKI reads the menu.

HIDEKI: We have to have rock shrimp tempura with ponzu.

HELEN: I'm with you there.

LILY: Ask him about the rape of Nanking.

HELEN looks at LILY.

HELEN: That will be a fantastic conversational topic, a guaranteed prelude to romance.

LILY: Ask him.

HELEN looks at LILY.

LILY: Please… You owe me.

HIDEKI: What are you thinking?

HELEN: About… the rape of Nanking.

HIDEKI: …I meant food. I was thinking… the black cod with miso?

HELEN: Sounds good… Recently I've become obsessed with East Asian, our history. I only really learned European history at school.

HIDEKI: Interesting… I've heard of it but I don't know what it's about.

HELEN looks at him in shock.

HELEN: But you learned history in school.

HIDEKI: Sure. I have an almost photographic memory when it comes to remembering dates. The time I really loved was the samurai era.

LILY: Ask him about the comfort women.

HELEN: Popo, I might… like him. We have a lot in common.

LILY: Do you want the next piece of the story or not?

Pause.

HELEN: Did you learn about comfort women?

HIDEKI looks at her.

HELEN: Young girls from China and Korea who were raped /
by Japanese…

HIDEKI shrinks back.

HIDEKI: /What is it with you and rape? Is that your thing?…
Are you one of those '*Fifty Shades*' girls?

HELEN: No.

HIDEKI: Rape is a pretty strong word. There's been a recent
article about the comfort women. There's proof that they
were paid prostitutes. Japan has nothing to be ashamed of.

LILY: I was here. I was here in Hong Kong lived through the
occupation.

HELEN: What about the Japanese occupation of Hong Kong?

HIDEKI: What about it?

LILY: I saw… and I can never un-see however much I might
want to.

HIDEKI sees LILY for the first time.

HIDEKI: I'm proud to be Japanese. Proud of our history.

LILY: To you we were animals, less than human. Our lives
didn't matter. The cobbles ran red with blood, bodies of
Chinese men, women and children lay piled up in the
streets.

HIDEKI: Our countries were at war.

LILY: The Japanese never apologised, accused us of lying. You need to own up to what you did.

HIDEKI: Me personally? I wasn't even alive.

HIDEKI puts money on the table.

HIDEKI: That's for the drinks.

He looks at HELEN.

HIDEKI: For a moment I thought we might have something, imagined us happy together.

HIDEKI exits.

LILY: *(Calling after him.)* I won't let you erase history.

HELEN turns on LILY.

HELEN: Hypocrite… I don't know my history. You denied me my story, denied me my …self.

LILY: I tried to protect /you.

HELEN: /No. You don't get to pretend that it was for my benefit. It was for you.

LILY looks at HELEN.

LILY: You want all of the story?

HELEN: Yes.

LILY: You don't know what you're asking for.

HELEN: I need it.

LILY nods, breathes and allows the dark memories to surface.

Steam fills the theatre.

The sound of metal cogs whirring.

The high-pitched sound of a child screaming in pain.

HELEN and LILY both cry out, react as if their right hand has been plunged into a vat of boiling water.

VOICE OF FACTORY FOREMAN: *(In Cantonese.)* How dare you fall asleep?

VOICE OF LILY CHILD: *(In Cantonese.)* Sorry, I didn't mean to. I passed out.

VOICE OF FACTORY FOREMAN: Do you know how many children want this job? I have to do this.

VOICE OF LILY CHILD: Yes.

VOICE OF FACTORY FOREMAN: *(In Cantonese.)* Have to make an example of you.

LILY: All my life I've been small, female, poor, powerless. My mother stood by silently and watched when my hand was forced into boiling water as punishment in the silk factory.

HELEN and LILY breathe through the pain.

LILY: A rich man had my father murdered and the system stole my inheritance, but I'm still here and I own my memories. I will speak out and pass them on however painful.

LILY faints, HELEN screams.

The light shifts, as if we were in a dream.

A JAPANESE SOLDIER enters, walks towards HELEN.

JAPANESE SOLDIER: *(In Japanese.)* Keep your eyes down dog.

HELEN keeps looking straight at him, she isn't afraid. The JAPANESE SOLDIER hits her hard around the face, she falls onto the table. He looks at her, rips her dress. HELEN struggles.

HELEN: No. Stop.

The JAPANESE SOLDIER hits her again. Now she is scared, he likes seeing her fear, feeds off it.

HELEN: Please.

LILY comes to, watches the scene, re-lives the past.

The JAPANESE SOLDIER exposes HELEN's breasts.

LILY: *(To HELEN.)* Repeat what I say. *(In Japanese.)* Stop.

The JAPANESE SOLDIER forces HELEN's legs apart, opens his flies.

HELEN: *(In English.)* Stop.

The JAPANESE SOLDIER stops, surprised.

LILY: *(In Japanese.)* Imagine if I was your sister.

HELEN: *(In English.)* Imagine if I was your sister.

The JAPANESE SOLDIER looks at HELEN in shock, she becomes human to him.

LILY: *(In Japanese.)* Are you not ashamed of yourself?

HELEN: *(In English.)* Aren't you ashamed of yourself?

The JAPANESE SOLDIER pushes HELEN away, closes his flies and exits.

LILY moves over to HELEN, takes her in her arms, tries to cover where her dress is torn.

HELEN breathes.

HELEN: Did that happen?

LILY: Yes.

HELEN: But he didn't…

LILY: No. I spoke up.

HELEN: In Japanese?

LILY: Yes.

HELEN: How did you learn Japanese?

LILY: I learned to speak a little during the War.

HELEN: So… the nightmare's over, you spoke to him and…

LILY: No.

A flickering light on another part of the stage. A Chinese prisoner crawls on his hands and knees. The JAPANESE SOLDIER circles him, beats him with a wooden stick, kicks him with his heavy black boots. The light flickers off, the sound of screams in the blackness.

LILY: It's only just beginning. There are Chinese prisoners. The Japanese need a translator.

HELEN looks at her, backs away, shakes her head.

LILY: Do you want to live?

The light flickers on. The JAPANESE SOLDIER makes the prisoner kneel, forces the wooden stick inside his knee joints.

LILY: You will translate forced confessions… work with the Japanese against your own people.

HELEN looks at the kneeling prisoner.

HELEN: I don't understand.

LILY: It cuts off the circulation, after an hour he'll be lame. It's agony.

The prisoner moans.

HELEN: No.

LILY: Whatever it takes… you must live.

The light flickers off.

HELEN: I… I want him to talk.

LILY: Most will after a couple of hours.

The prisoner moans from the shadows.

HELEN: And if he doesn't?

The light flickers back on. The prisoner is still kneeling.

LILY: They'll force a tube down his throat, pump water into his stomach, blow him up like a balloon. They'll place a plank on top force the water out of every orifice. Many died. I have nightmares… Can't unsee…

HELEN looks away.

LILY: Don't you dare look away. You forced me to come back here.

HELEN looks at the prisoner who throws himself out of his position.

PRISONER: *(In Cantonese.)* I confess. I'm guilty.

The JAPANESE SOLDIER draws out a long sword, raises it.

HELEN: I can't... I can't...

The light flickers off. HELEN is crying, she retches. LILY holds HELEN.

LILY: It's alright. It's alright. We can stop, you don't have to carry on.

LILY rocks HELEN like a child.

HELEN: No. We can't stop. This is what you lived through. This is what happened. If you could bear it so can I. We have to go on.

INTERVAL.

At Sea

1.

LILY stands in a kitchen. Light falls through a porthole. There is a sense of movement, of being in-between worlds.

LILY chops and deseeds three chillis.

HELEN enters, looks around her.

HELEN: Where are we?

LILY: Aboard the SS Canton.

> *LILY takes a couple of stalks of lemongrass, bashes them.*

HELEN: On our way to…?

LILY: England.

HELEN: Home.

LILY: …Yes, for you.

> *LILY inhales the smell of the lemongrass and then chops the stalks.*

LILY: There's nothing for me to do. I find my way down to the kitchens.

> *KIT YE enters, stylish and fabulous, she holds an ice cream cone, offers it to LILY.*

KIT YE: Taste? I haven't licked this side.

> *LILY declines, chops six spring onions.*

HELEN: Auntie Kit?

KIT YE: Have we met?

> *HELEN looks at LILY.*

HELEN: Yes… but not yet?

LILY: This is Helen my granddaughter.

KIT YE: I knew I shouldn't have had that second glass of wine.

LILY chops fresh coriander.

HELEN: You're exactly how I imagined you as a young woman.

KIT YE: Lily's granddaughter… Is time travel involved?

HELEN: Something like that.

The sound of a knife falling.

HELEN: Even now you two are similar.

KIT YE: Chinese women of a certain age with shadowy pasts.

HELEN looks at her.

KIT YE: Well honestly, you don't get on a boat and travel half way around the world if things are going well do you?

HELEN: No. I suppose not.

HELEN glances at LILY who has paused.

HELEN: Ginger?

LILY nods, peels and chops ginger.

HELEN: I know what you're making.

LILY: I create my green chicken curry on this boat.

HELEN: I know.

LILY: I experiment with new ingredients we pick up along the way.

LILY smashes garlic cloves with the back of a cleaver, discards the skin, chops it.

HELEN: Coconut from Malaysia for a smooth base. In the Bay of Bengal you stir in a little self-raising flour to make it lighter and creamier. In India you perfect the mix of spices.

LILY: Correct.

LILY takes a large stone mortar, places the chopped chillies, lemongrass, spring onions, coriander, ginger and garlic inside. She grinds the mixture with a pestle.

HELEN: Lily Kwok's famous green chicken curry. The cornerstone of Lung Fung.

The aroma fills the theatre.

KIT YE: What's Lung Fung?

LILY adds shrimp paste and salt.

LILY: My restaurant.

KIT YE: You succeed? You open a restaurant?

Pause.

HELEN: Yes. She does.

LILY adds brown sugar.

KIT YE: *(To HELEN.)* We sit on deck eating strawberry ice creams staring out at the horizon dreaming of one day owning our own businesses.

LILY zests a lime, cuts it and squeezes in the juice.

HELEN: She never talks about it but in Middleton… Lung Fung is legendary. Everything I've heard about it is from customers who still miss it.

LILY adds vegetable oil and pepper.

KIT YE: What happened to it?

LILY pounds the mixture violently with the pestle. The obsessive rhythmic clack of mahjong tiles.

HELEN: Popo, tell us from the beginning.

The seductive clack of the mahjong tiles.

KIT YE: What's that? What fun! Shall we play?

LILY: NO.

The sound of the mahjong tiles fades.

HELEN: It was the first Chinese restaurant in Middleton. There hasn't been another restaurant like it. Why the name? Why Lung Fung?

LILY: Dragon and phoenix.

KIT YE: Rebirth?

LILY: Yes. I dream up the name on this boat. I work for the Woodmans in England for five years, save. *(To KIT YE.)* You end up in Manchester… It seems as good a place as any.

I find an old shop in a Victorian terrace in Middleton.

LILY fires up the stove and heats a wok.

HELEN: And you just know?

LILY: Yes. It's the window… It has a wide front window and I can imagine standing outside looking in.

LILY adds a little oil.

HELEN: The women in silk dresses and red lipstick enjoying your food.

LILY: I can see it even though the building's a wreck. I have to scrub out every inch.

LILY adds the curry paste to the hot oil, stirs. The smell fills the theatre.

HELEN: On your own?

LILY: Yes.

KIT YE: Don't I help?

LILY: You're going to but something comes up.

HELEN: And you manage?

LILY: Yes. You just do whatever needs to be done, work sixteen, eighteen hour days. It's not easy making something out of nothing.

HELEN: Go on.

LILY opens a can of coconut milk, adds it to the wok, stirs the paste into the milk.

LILY: I know I want Lung Fung to be a place where everyone is welcome. I know if the food's good, the portions generous and it's affordable… people will come back.

LILY adds chicken to the wok.

HELEN: And they do?

LILY: Yes. After a year I start to see a little profit.

KIT YE: And your customers are local people?

LILY nods.

HELEN: I heard pop stars flocked to Lung Fung.

KIT YE: No!

LILY: They come later… It's the women who make Lung Fung a success. Most of them work in the factories. After a long, hard day they still have to feed their families.

LILY adds Chinese leaf, carrots, bamboo shoots and water chestnuts to the wok, stirs.

HELEN: Cooking from scratch.

LILY: I keep my prices low so they treat themselves. Allow the weekly luxury of being cooked for.

HELEN: How do you keep them low?

LILY: For the first year I work alone *(to HELEN)* and then with your mother.

KIT YE: You bring Mabel to England?

LILY: Eventually.

KIT YE: Bravo.

LILY stirs the curry.

HELEN: And is this on the menu from the start?

LILY: Yes. I write the daily menus up on a blackboard, draw a line down the middle.

HELEN: Why?

LILY: An English menu on one side.

KIT YE: What's on it?

LILY: Lamb chop

KIT YE makes a face.

KIT YE: Lovely.

LILY: With vegetables or chicken and chips.

HELEN: And on the Chinese side?

LILY: This chicken curry with rice and beef chow mein.

HELEN: Which menu is most popular?

LILY: At first… well, people stick to what they know. But I keep making special offers on the Chinese side. Sometimes people need a nudge. In time they get a taste for our food.

LILY dips a piece of bread into the curry, blows on it, offers it to KIT YE who tastes it. KIT YE makes a sound of pure pleasure.

LILY: Lung Fung is the place to be.

HELEN: You bring Hong Kong to Middleton.

LILY: I have to, cooking, the smell, the taste… I keep Hong Kong with me, hold onto myself.

KIT YE claps with admiration.

KIT YE: You're a success.

LILY: Yes... I achieve... what for years had seemed impossible. I live with my daughter, have a thriving business. I have money. Life's good.

KIT YE: And then?

The obsessive rhythmic clack of mahjong tiles.

LILY: I fuck up.

HELEN: Popo!

LILY turns off the stove, looks at HELEN.

LILY: I'll tell you once and never again.

A strip light switches on above a mahjong table, three PLAYERS seated, drinking and smoking. The mahjong tiles are placed face down, the tiles are shuffled: an obsessive, seductive, rhythmic sound.

LILY: Kit.

LILY indicates and KIT YE takes her place at the mahjong table, rolls the dice. They start to play.

LILY steels herself, she fixes her hair, applies red lipstick, she sheds a layer revealing a 60's dress.

LILY: I'd worked like a dog and worried, endless sleepless nights, for ten years to build my business.

HELEN glances at LILY.

HELEN: Do you want me to be you?

LILY: No. Not this time.

The game picks up speed. The rhythmic clack of the mahjong tiles.

LILY makes an entrance.

PLAYER 2 pushes his winning sets forward on the table, leaps into the air. The other PLAYERS laugh and applaud him.

The PROPRIETRESS gets up and approaches LILY.

PROPRIETRESS: Lily Kwok?

LILY: Have we met before?

PROPRIETRESS: No. Everyone knows Lily Kwok the owner of the legendary Lung Fung. Welcome.

The PROPRIETRESS leads her to the table.

PLAYER 2: *(To the PROPRIETRESS.)* Champagne all around.

KIT YE stands up, hugs LILY.

KIT YE: This is my dear friend Lily Kwok.

LILY: Hello.

PLAYER 1: I've heard about you and your restaurant.

PLAYER 2: Do you know how to play?

LILY: A little. Kit taught me to play on the boat coming over.

KIT YE: Guilty as charged.

LILY and KIT are fabulous and admired. The PROPRIETRESS opens a bottle of champagne. LILY is startled. LILY and KIT laugh.

PLAYER 2: Come on new girl, show us what you've got.

LILY rolls the dice. They start to play. LILY can't keep up, loses.

PLAYER 1: Better luck next time.

The PROPRIETRESS hands LILY a glass of champagne.

LILY: It doesn't matter. I'm having fun.

LILY drinks champagne, feels like she belongs. The PROPRIETRESS tops up her glass.

LILY: Again.

LILY rolls the dice.

They start to play. The game picks up speed. The clack of the mahjong tiles, the intensity and concentration.

LILY cries out, pushes her winning sets forward on the table.

The PROPRIETRESS pours her more champagne.

PROPRIETRESS: Congratulations.

KIT YE: Well played darling.

The PROPRIETRESS hands her a stack of notes. LILY shuffles through the notes, looks at KIT.

LILY: Four-hundred pounds for nothing.

KIT YE: Let me see that.

KIT YE takes the money, counts it, cries out.

LILY: Let's make a new rule. Money we win, we can spend, we don't have to save it.

KIT YE: No. Won't put it away for a rainy day.

LILY: Won't put it back into the business. Tomorrow we'll go into Manchester and have our hair done, then we'll buy new outfits.

KIT YE: Fabulous.

PLAYER 1: Aren't you both. Can I come?

KIT YE: Girls only.

LILY: We'll see you Friday night here at the table.

PLAYER 1: 'Til then.

The PLAYERS move places. KIT YE steps out, lights a cigarette.

LILY is confident, a success, she is going to win.

LILY rolls the dice and they start to play. The playing becomes faster and more intense through KIT's speech. The obsessive rhythmic clack of the mahjong tiles.

KIT YE: Lily goes to the Palace Friday nights after closing. She's lucky… at first. She comes home in the early morning high from excitement and winning. She looks forward to

Fridays, on a Wednesday night she thinks, just two more days, then that thought moves to Tuesday, to Monday.

PLAYER 2 wins.

LILY rolls the dice again. They start to play. This time there's desperation in LILY's playing.

KIT YE: She starts closing early on a Friday. Then on other days. She loses interest in …everything. All she can think about is being at the Palace, winning.

The PROPRIETRESS wins.

KIT YE: She works full shifts at Lung Fung, drives into Manchester and gambles all night. She drinks endless black coffee, lives on adrenaline.

PLAYER 1 wins.

KIT YE: Go home Lily.

LILY: No.

LILY rolls the dice again, starts another game. They play furiously.

LILY: I created… I dreamed of being an amah and I became one. I dreamed of opening a restaurant, I have and it's exceeded my wildest dreams. I'm a success. That belief… I can see it… I'll borrow money from loan sharks, a little, then some more. I won't take half measures… know my luck will turn…

PLAYER 1 wins. The other PLAYERS leave. LILY sits alone at the mahjong table.

The PROPRIETRESS starts to close up, doesn't meet LILY's eye.

LILY: There's no question of not re-paying the loans.

HELEN: Triads?

LILY: Yes.

The PROPRIETRESS stacks the chairs.

KIT YE: You can sell the car, the furniture.

LILY: It's no use.

HELEN: There must be something we can do.

LILY: Lung Fung has to go.

Pause.

HELEN: But you worked so hard.

LILY: ...Don't question tragedy and learn from my mistakes. That's why I'm telling you...

HELEN: You deserve to be happy.

LILY: Gambling is the Chinese curse, don't ever start, this is where it leads.

HELEN: Why? Why would you be so self destructive? I don't understand.

The sound of a baby crying. LILY ignores it.

KIT YE: Ah Bing?

HELEN: Who?

KIT YE: You don't know all of the story, you can't possibly understand.

HELEN looks at LILY.

HELEN: Still? You're still holding back?

LILY: You didn't much like the war.

HELEN: Who does? But it's still a part of my story, part of me. You forced me to see and I'm glad. You made me ...stronger.

They look at each other.

KIT YE: *(To LILY.)* You need to tell her. *(To HELEN.)* You have to go back to Hong Kong.

2.

The sound of a baby crying.

An old fashioned perambulator rolls onstage.

HELEN: Is this…?

LILY: It's baby Catherine, Catherine Woodman.

HELEN goes over to the perambulator and picks up the baby.

HELEN: *(To LILY.)* Ambition fulfilled, a white baby.

HELEN cuddles the baby. LILY starts to sing a Cantonese lullaby, HELEN joins in, the two sing to the baby who stops crying and goes to sleep.

MRS WOODMAN comes home from a party.

MRS WOODMAN: What pretty singing.

MRS WOODMAN sways slightly.

MRS WOODMAN: How is she?

MRS WOODMAN moves closer.

MRS WOODMAN: How long has she been asleep?

HELEN: I just got her off.

MRS WOODMAN: You're wonderful with babies, know exactly what to do.

MRS WOODMAN softly strokes the baby.

MRS WOODMAN: What's she wearing?

HELEN: A dress I made her, white cotton with tiny pink rosebuds. I sewed lace around the hem and neck, stitched a backing in so it doesn't itch.

HELEN puts the baby back in the perambulator.

HELEN: It's late I'd better say good night.

MRS WOODMAN: Good night.

MRS WOODMAN hiccups.

MRS WOODMAN: Where do you have to get back to?

HELEN: Wan Chai.

MRS WOODMAN: What's it like?

HELEN: ...Very different to here. Another world.

MRS WOODMAN: How long does it take to get there?

HELEN: Half an hour.

MRS WOODMAN: Imagine... you get to go to a different world in half an hour. Lucky you.

HELEN: Yes. Lucky me.

MRS WOODMAN: Is anyone waiting for you at home?

HELEN: My mother.

MRS WOODMAN: That's a Chinese custom, isn't it to live... generations together.

HELEN: She watches my daughter while I work.

HELEN looks at LILY. MRS WOODMAN looks at HELEN.

MRS WOODMAN: Oh... I didn't know. How old is she?

HELEN: A month older than Catherine.

Pause.

MRS WOODMAN: What's her name?

HELEN: Mabel.

MRS WOODMAN: Pretty. Why didn't you...?

They look at each other.

MRS WOODMAN: I shouldn't have kept you. Is Wan Chai safe at night?

HELEN: I walk quickly, keep my head down.

MRS WOODMAN: Good night.

HELEN: Good night.

HELEN exits.

3.

The sound of a baby crying: primal, full of need and desperation.

A slum room in Wan Chai, TAI PO sits on the floor, a bundle beside her.

HELEN enters, walks over to the bundle.

HELEN: I missed you.

HELEN kneels down by the bundle.

TAI PO: Don't wake her. She was hungry wouldn't stop crying, cried herself to sleep. Did you bring evaporated milk?

HELEN: Yes. Why didn't you buy some?

TAI PO looks down.

LILY: The housekeeping money?... Again?

HELEN looks at LILY who turns away.

HELEN: Have you eaten?

TAI PO: No.

HELEN takes a packet out of her pocket, gives it to TAI PO.

HELEN: Leftover cake and broken biscuits. I'm sorry, I wish it were rice.

TAI PO opens the waxed paper packet, eats.

HELEN: My milk's gone. I can't feed her.

Pause.

HELEN: I... ache when I'm away from her.

TAI PO: I hold her tight and add a little sugar to the evaporated milk. She's content, apart from…

HELEN: Was she hungry all day?

TAI PO: Yes. I tried to distract her. Took her for a walk to the harbour.

HELEN: She loves the boats.

TAI PO: All crammed with refugees from the mainland.

HELEN: Yes of course, terrifying what's…

TAI PO: Wan Chai can't take any more.

HELEN: It can it will it has to.

Pause.

TAI PO: She rolled over.

HELEN: When?

TAI PO: This afternoon.

TAI PO moves her hand making shadow animals.

TAI PO: She was reaching for my hand. She stretched out her little arm and then… Her eyes opened wide with surprise.

HELEN: My clever beautiful baby.

TAI PO looks at her sternly.

TAI PO: Lily.

HELEN: She is.

TAI PO: Don't bring her up with …expectations.

Pause.

LILY: At night I hold her. She wants to feed, gets upset.
I …mind too. But I hold her little body next to mine.
I made her, inside me, all my dreams, thoughts. Even
though I'm tired I'm happy when she wakes in the night…

HELEN: When I wake up, she's asleep. When I get home, she's asleep. I see her every other Sunday morning, that's all.

TAI PO: Be grateful for that.

HELEN nods.

TAI PO: Thankful for your job.

HELEN: I am.

TAI PO picks up the bundle.

TAI PO: You have what every woman in Wan Chai wants. The families of the amah's have ...security, don't have the constant stress of how they're going to pay their rent, where their next meal is coming from.

TAI PO exits. HELEN turns to LILY.

HELEN: Three generations eat because of you. You support your mother, my mother...

CHAN enters, he's been drinking.

HELEN: It's late.

CHAN: I was looking for work. Fucking refugees. Cockroaches.

HELEN: Don't say that.

CHAN moves towards her, goes to strike her. HELEN shrinks back.

CHAN: Don't you ever tell me what to do.

HELEN looks at LILY in shock.

HELEN: ...Sorry.

CHAN: Wages are half what they used to be because of them. I won't stand in line with vermin.

HELEN: Mabel went hungry today.

CHAN: So did I.

HELEN: You were the one who decided to...

CHAN: What?

HELEN: Drink my money.

CHAN looks at HELEN with contempt, pulls money out of his pocket and throws it at her.

HELEN kneels on the floor, picks up the money, counts it.

CHAN: It's all you care about, talk about. Christ you're boring.

HELEN: How did you get this?

CHAN: I won it.

HELEN: Gambling?

Pause.

CHAN: Do you think I like living off you? Think I don't know what people say?

HELEN: No one says anything.

CHAN: To you. But I hear... It hurts me to think of you... subservient.

CHAN looks around the squalid room.

CHAN: I don't want us to live like this.

HELEN: Me neither.

CHAN looks at her tenderly.

CHAN: I hate seeing you like this. I want to see you wearing a fine dress of ...green silk.

HELEN: Like when we met again that time, after the War.

CHAN: Yes.

They look at each other, stand still, frozen in time for a moment.

The light changes. Music plays.

CHAN breaks out of the stillness, drifts towards her, he is high. CHAN kisses her gently on the forehead.

CHAN: You're my wife.

HELEN: Yes.

CHAN reaches out to HELEN and dances with her.

CHAN: Your hair will be cut in a bob. You'll wear red lipstick, perfume of …tuberose.

CHAN spins her around and around.

CHAN: We'll have money… You'll walk pushing our baby in one of the western contraptions. Every man will look at you and be jealous. I'll walk beside you in a smart suit and be proud.

They move apart, holding both hands.

HELEN: Did Mabel eat today?

CHAN: Your eyes… You're doing that thing with your eyes.

CHAN lets go of HELEN and she falls backwards.

The light changes. The sound of MABEL crying, the sounds of the slums: dogs barking, a couple arguing in the street.

HELEN: He's mad… cruel.

LILY: The opium changed him, brought it out.

A light flickers on on another part of the stage. GONG singing (In Cantonese.) and dancing for an audience of admirers. GONG is thirty, a nightclub singer, she is beautiful, wears a green silk dress, red lipstick, her hair cut in a bob.

LILY stands staring at GONG, HELEN can't take her eyes off her either.

LILY: Tuberose… sickly, cloying. That's how I knew she'd been at my house with my husband and baby. They run up debts in my name. Men come round… There's no question of not paying.

CHAN brings GONG a drink, takes out a silver cigarette case, offers her a cigarette, lights it for her, looks at her with admiration. They flirt and laugh. CHAN leans towards her, they kiss.

LILY: I saw her… Gong, that was her name.

CHAN sees HELEN, walks towards her, stops.

HELEN: I work and you… it all goes on drink, opium, gambling, Gong.

Music plays softly, GONG starts to dance.

CHAN: Come here.

HELEN stands still.

CHAN: Come here. Now.

HELEN moves towards him slowly. He looks at her with contempt.

CHAN: I wish you could see yourself. Wait.

CHAN takes out his silver cigarette case, glances at his reflection, he's high. He holds it up to HELEN.

CHAN: Look.

HELEN looks warily at CHAN, then looks at her reflection.

CHAN: Tell me. What do you see?

HELEN: I don't… I don't recognise myself.

LILY turns away.

CHAN: I see nothing. I see nothing special. Say it.

HELEN shakes her head.

CHAN: Look at you and then look at Gong.

HELEN looks at GONG smiling and dancing.

HELEN: Leaving you is all I think about.

CHAN: What's stopping you?

HELEN: ...A woman with a child, an elderly mother and no money.

CHAN moves towards her, the threat of violence, he is out of control.

CHAN: Say it.

HELEN: I'm nothing, nothing special.

CHAN nods.

CHAN: Now do you understand why I'd want to be with someone like Gong? I tried but... No one could ever love you Lily.

GONG looks over at HELEN, CHAN walks back towards her.

LILY turns and forces herself to look at CHAN and GONG together.

LILY: There was never anyone else. I did love him. For a while, he was my world. That short time was probably the happiest of my life. I meant what I said...

LILY looks at CHAN.

LILY: *(In Cantonese and repeated in English.)* 'When I'm with you. I belong. I'm home.'

Pause.

HELEN: But now... you leave him.

LILY: Yes. I can't afford to be stupid anymore.

HELEN: It's over.

LILY looks at HELEN.

HELEN: The nightmare's over.

LILY: No. Not yet. I'm pregnant again.

4.

HELEN stands in the large old fashioned kitchen. She is heavily pregnant, rests one hand on her stomach. MRS WOODMAN enters.

MRS WOODMAN: Is there something you should tell me?

HELEN looks up startled.

MRS WOODMAN: Congratulations! I'm very happy for you.

HELEN: …Thank you.

MRS WOODMAN: I thought so but I couldn't be sure.
You hide it very well. New life is …precious.

HELEN: …Yes.

MRS WOODMAN: A little brother or sister for Mabel. Your husband must be thrilled. Hoping for a boy I suspect.

HELEN: Of course.

MRS WOODMAN looks at her kindly.

MRS WOODMAN: You need to look after yourself Lily, get enough rest.

HELEN looks at her.

HELEN: I was wondering if I could take a little time off?

MRS WOODMAN: Of course you must. When are you due?

HELEN: Next month.

MRS WOODMAN: You must stop working today.

MRS WOODMAN sits down.

MRS WOODMAN: Come and sit down.

HELEN sits with MRS WOODMAN.

MRS WOODMAN: I want you to take at least three months off.

LILY gives HELEN a look.

HELEN: Two will be plenty.

MRS WOODMAN: No. Spend time with your baby. I met a new sort of doctor, a psychologist, at a dinner last week and he said that apparently it's important.

HELEN looks at MRS WOODMAN.

HELEN: Shall I contact the agency for you?

MRS WOODMAN: No that won't be necessary.

HELEN: But you won't be able to manage without…

MRS WOODMAN: I'll call them myself. Explain exactly what I'm looking for.

HELEN: A month will be enough.

MRS WOODMAN looks at HELEN.

MRS WOODMAN: I'll tell them that I need a temporary while you're on leave.

LILY: Thank you.

MRS WOODMAN: I couldn't manage without you. Your job will be waiting for you when you're ready to come back.

HELEN turns to LILY.

HELEN: Maternity pay?

LILY: Doesn't exist. She's being extremely kind.

HELEN turns back to MRS WOODMAN.

HELEN: Thank you. You don't know how much this means to me.

MRS WOODMAN smiles graciously and exits.

HELEN touches her swollen stomach.

HELEN: I didn't know about…

LILY: No.

HELEN: Does the baby ...survive?

LILY: Second births are much ...easier. She comes quickly.

HELEN: She?

LILY: Ah Bing... I don't not love her. I don't not want...

LILY turns away from HELEN.

LILY: I don't know when we'll eat. My mother never eats, gives everything to Mabel and I look at Mabel's face see she's so hungry she's in pain and I can't do anything. Money... I don't have any money.

Pause.

LILY: My milk doesn't last long. Ah Bing doesn't stop crying. All she knows of life is hunger, distress. I wish... I wish she'd chosen a different mother. But... I love her. She is... me. I grew her in my body, didn't give her enough hope... there isn't...

LILY takes a breath, takes control of herself.

LILY: I beg in the street with Ah Bing strapped to my back. I want to die. I don't. I keep us all alive.

Pause.

LILY: I keep bleeding. I go back to the hospital even though I can't pay. I beg the doctor to help me. He suggests I meet with a patient of his.

5.

MRS LEE enters. She is Chinese in her forties and extremely elegant, the kind of elegance that only comes with wealth.

HELEN and LILY look at her.

MRS LEE: Lily?

LILY draws back.

HELEN: Mrs Lee?

MRS LEE: Hello.

An awkward silence.

MRS LEE: Oh… this is difficult.

HELEN: Yes.

Pause.

MRS LEE: How are you?

HELEN: Fine… No not fine.

They look at each other.

MRS LEE: Let's not make small talk.

HELEN: No.

Pause.

MRS LEE: My husband and I have tried for years…
We haven't been blessed. I've been pregnant five times
but have never managed to…

Pause.

MRS LEE: There's a nursery in our house. I had it decorated
the first time I… It's a blue grey, like the sea. I painted fish
and sea creatures, cut them out and put them on the walls.
I thought… when this little one's inside me it must be like
being a sea creature. I wanted him or her to be at home on
the earth with me after… The door to that room's locked.
I never go in there. Every day it hurts… The ache goes …
very deep. I've been to numerous doctors, acupuncturists,
herbalists, fertility specialists… I would understand if my
husband were to take a second wife. I've failed… I'm not a
woman.

HELEN: No. Don't say that, please…

MRS LEE: He hasn't. He loves me. He deserves to be... I must have been to every fortune teller in Hong Kong, lit incense and prayed at every shrine but no one's listening.
I even visited shamans.

HELEN reaches out to MRS LEE.

LILY: She's called Ah Bing, she's three weeks old... I love her.

HELEN looks at LILY.

HELEN: Doesn't your husband want a boy?

MRS LEE: No... No... It doesn't matter to us. He's... He's an extraordinary man, not traditional in that sense. We... are desperate for a baby. We've almost given up hope.

HELEN glances at LILY.

HELEN: If I could keep her I would but I can't see how...
I love her. It isn't possible to carry a baby for nine months and not...

MRS LEE: I know.

HELEN: I'm... I can't see a future for myself, for my daughter, for this baby.

They look at each other.

HELEN: Will you love her even though she isn't your blood?

MRS LEE: Yes. She will be our longed for daughter.

HELEN hands MRS LEE a small photograph of Ah Bing. MRS LEE looks at the photograph.

HELEN: I... I want...

MRS LEE looks at HELEN.

MRS LEE: We will do anything to... be parents to Ah Bing. Can we help you ...financially?

LILY: No.

HELEN: I want to be an …aunt, be allowed a little …contact.

MRS LEE: Yes of course. I'm… I can never….

LILY: Two more days.

HELEN: Give me two more days with Ah Bing.

Pause.

HELEN: Don't worry I won't change my mind. On Friday I'll bring her to your house and say goodbye. What's your address?

MRS LEE: Sixty-one Robinson Road.

HELEN: Chinese live on Robinson Road?

MRS LEE: We do. We might be the first.

HELEN: I'll be there on Friday by noon.

HELEN and MRS LEE look at each other, MRS LEE exits. HELEN reaches out to hold LILY but LILY moves away.

LILY: No. Let's just get through to the end.

6.

A dingy slum room in Wan Chai. MRS WOODMAN enters carrying a present tied with a bow. She covers her mouth and nose with a silk scarf, tears come to her eyes as she looks around.

MRS WOODMAN waits. A noise from outside.

MRS WOODMAN: *(Calling out.)* Lily?

LILY nods at HELEN who walks into the sordid room.

MRS WOODMAN: Sorry I should have… Fridays I always have lunch at the Ritz and it's close by… I thought I'd…

MRS WOODMAN holds out the present tied with a bow.

MRS WOODMAN: For the baby.

Numb, HELEN takes it.

MRS WOODMAN: Aren't you going to open it?

HELEN unties the ribbon and opens the present, inside baby clothes.

MRS WOODMAN: I went through Catherine's old things, picked out the nicest.

MRS WOODMAN holds up a little dress.

MRS WOODMAN: Look isn't this darling with the pink rosebuds and lace, you made it for her remember?

MRS WOODMAN hands the dress to HELEN.

MRS WOODMAN: Oh… Is it a boy? There are lots of whites, neutrals.

HELEN turns away.

MRS WOODMAN: What… What's the matter?

MRS WOODMAN looks around the room.

MRS WOODMAN: Where's…? Did something…?

MRS WOODMAN looks at HELEN's stricken face.

MRS WOODMAN: Oh my darling… I'm sorry…

Pause.

HELEN: Please… I didn't want you to come here, to see this.

MRS WOODMAN: I'm glad I came and saw …real life. I don't think any the less of you.

HELEN: …I'm married to a man addicted to… whatever he can lay his hands on. He gambles, spends my money on whores.

MRS WOODMAN looks at HELEN.

MRS WOODMAN: Well, that happens… You're a good person Lily. I know you.

HELEN: I can't see a way out.

MRS WOODMAN: I'm your friend.

HELEN looks at MRS WOODMAN.

LILY: Tell her.

HELEN: The baby didn't die. I gave her away... To a Chinese woman, desperate for a baby, she has money... Ah Bing deserves more than... What sort of a life can I give her? Look at how I live.

MRS WOODMAN looks around the sordid room.

MRS WOODMAN: What you've done is a true act of love. Completely unselfish.

HELEN nods, MRS WOODMAN takes her hand.

MRS WOODMAN: We're leaving Hong Kong, going back to England.

HELEN looks at her, fights rising panic.

MRS WOODMAN: Would you like to come with us?

Pause.

HELEN: To England?

MRS WOODMAN: Yes... You don't have to decide right now... We think of you as one of the family. I want to help you, give you a chance in a richer country.

HELEN: ...I'd be free of him.

MRS WOODMAN: You'll live with us. We'll pay you English wages.

HELEN: I'll send money home.

MRS WOODMAN: And save Lily, save. For your future, for Mabel's. One day you'll be able to bring her over.

HELEN: To England?

MRS WOODMAN: Of course.

HELEN: She'll be English?

MRS WOODMAN: Yes, in time. Think it over. I know it's a big decision.

MRS WOODMAN exits. HELEN turns to LILY.

HELEN: /Yes.

LILY: /Yes.

HELEN: It's not too late. I'll run to Robinson Road, tell Mrs Lee I've changed my mind. The circumstances have changed. Ah Bing is my daughter.

Pause.

LILY: I don't.

HELEN: Why?

LILY: I can't take her with me.

Pause.

LILY: Does your mother ever talk about her childhood?

HELEN: No.

LILY: There's a reason for that.

Pause.

LILY: All my life I told myself that I didn't have a choice but I did. There's always a... I didn't have to work with the Japanese.

HELEN: They would have tortured you, killed you.

LILY: ...There was still a choice.

HELEN: In your shoes, I made the same decision.

LILY: Would you have given Ah Bing away?

Pause.

HELEN: No.

LEUNG appears, carrying a small battered cardboard suitcase.

LEUNG: The problem was there were two mountains that stood in the way.

HELEN: I can understand…

LEUNG: The villagers laughed and mocked him said, 'how stupid you are. How can one old man move two entire mountains?'

HELEN: *(To LILY.)* You used to tell me this story. The old man replied, 'though I shall die, /I shall leave behind my daughter and my daughter's daughters. Since the mountains cannot grow taller I see no reason why we won't be able to level them.' After five generations…

LEUNG: / I shall leave behind my daughter and my daughter's daughters. Since the mountains cannot grow taller I see no reason why we won't be able to level them.' After five generations…

LILY: STOP.

LILY turns on LEUNG.

LILY: I wish you had never told me this story.

LILY breaks down.

LILY: Wish you hadn't burdened me with your …ambition.

LEUNG: Don't get lost in the past, never question it. Move forwards, upwards. You know what you have to do.

LEUNG leaves the suitcase at LILY's feet and exits.

LILY: But what about the daughter's daughters?

HELEN: I don't…

LILY: They were too young didn't have a choice, I decided for them and they suffered… and all because I was determined to walk amongst the white people as their equal.

HELEN: And we do.

LILY: The cost… the cost was too high.

LILY sobs.

7.

The light changes. The sound of the sea. There is a sense of movement, of being in-between worlds.

LILY and HELEN stand on deck.

LILY: Leaving Hong Kong part of me dies.

HELEN looks at her.

LILY: You can't just transplant… things are always lost.

HELEN: Does anyone come to see you off?

LILY: No.

They look out at Hong Kong fading into the distance.

LILY: I promise Mabel I'll send for her as soon as I can, as soon as I've saved enough money for her fare. She's three when I leave. Too young to understand time… A long time… she imagines a week, two maybe three…

Pause.

LILY: I know it will be years.

HELEN looks at LILY.

LILY: It's dark when I leave. She's sleeping. I kiss her on the forehead, breathe in her baby smell: new skin and clean hair… I love watching her sleep… That's always our special time in the early morning… before I leave for…

A kitchen appears. Light falls through a porthole, the kitchen shifts, rocks.

HELEN takes a cleaver and skilfully cuts up and disjoints a chicken.

LILY: I know I have to go to England, change the story of our family.

The cleaver slices through the chicken.

LILY: But leaving…

Each strike a decisive severance.

LILY: My ancestors waited lifetimes for opportunities that never came.

The following speech is punctuated by the rhythm of the blade slicing the chicken and hitting the board.

LILY: My first… I was able to become an amah… I leave Hong Kong when I'm thirty-five… I worked and waited twenty-three years for that next …chance.

Pause.

LILY: I see it for what it is. Know I have to…

LILY puts rice into a pan, pours in water and washes the rice.

LILY: When I think about… Feel… When I get lost inside… /I work.

HELEN: /I cook.

LILY: Work until I feel the ache in my body. Bring myself back to what's real.

HELEN: Garlic, ginger, onion, spring onions.

HELEN gathers together ingredients.

LILY: Four generations. We do it in four.

HELEN: The mountains?

LILY: What else? I want to do it in three but… They level when you graduate and become a lawyer.

HELEN: Popo… Becoming a lawyer…

HELEN reaches for a Chinese sausage.

LILY: Lap cheong. I know what you're making.

HELEN: Mum used to make this for me whenever I felt sad.

LILY nods, puts the rice on. HELEN peels a garlic clove, smashes it with the side of the cleaver, chops it.

LILY: Six years later I come back to Hong Kong to collect your mother.

HELEN: Six years?

LILY nods, scrapes the skin off the ginger with a cleaver.

LILY: I've missed her. Thought about her every day, worked and saved every penny.

HELEN: She must have missed you too.

LILY shakes her head, chops the ginger.

LILY: She doesn't remember me. We're strangers.

The light shifts with the movement of the boat.

LILY: Hong Kong is all she knows and something breaks when she leaves.

LILY peels an onion, cuts the skin off in quarters, stares into space.

LILY: How was school?

HELEN glances sideways at LILY, chops a spring onion.

VOICE OF MABEL CHILD: *(In Cantonese.)* Terrible.

LILY: Speak English. You have to be English.

LILY chops the onion. The sound of two blades falling.

VOICE OF MABEL CHILD: *(In English with a Cantonese accent.)* School fine.

LILY: …Good. You're lucky to go to school. Why are you dirty? Your clothes torn, your hair all messed up?

VOICE OF MABEL CHILD: *(In English.)* You know why.

LILY: You have to stand up to them.

VOICE OF MABEL CHILD: *(In English.)* No. Too many. Not strong enough.

HELEN chops the lap cheong.

LILY: Where was I?

HELEN hands her Chinese cabbage.

LILY: Yes. That's it.

LILY breathes, shreds Chinese cabbage.

LILY: This is what I make her when she aches for home, for Hong Kong, for my mother. I'm strict don't allow her to cry.

HELEN: Why?

LILY shakes her head.

LILY: I feed her claypot chicken. It comforts her.

HELEN: It comforts me.

HELEN heats a wok over a high flame, adds oil.

LILY: And me… I lie in bed at night and picture Wan Chai. I see it in such vivid colours I can smell it, feel the humidity… over time the pictures get fainter until I can't see…

HELEN holds the back of her hand above the wok to check the heat, puts garlic into a metal ladle and adds it to the wok, adds ginger, onion, spring onion and lap cheong, stirs with the metal ladle.

LILY: Now I can… I see it again through your eyes.

The smell of cooking fills the theatre.

91

LILY: Thoughts are repetitive, circular… and underneath…

HELEN: Underneath?

LILY: The ache.

A moment of recognition between them.

LILY: I thought Ah Bing would have a better life with the Lees.

HELEN: And does she?

Pause.

LILY takes the wooden spatula from HELEN, stirs. The smell of cooking fills the theatre.

LILY adds water, a pinch of salt, a teaspoon of sugar.

HELEN: Oyster sauce.

LILY adds oyster sauce.

LILY: Sesame oil.

HELEN adds sesame oil, it's a game they've played since HELEN was little.

HELEN: Dark soy.

LILY adds soy.

LILY: Shaoxing rice wine.

HELEN adds the rice wine. The way they cook together is like dancing, they finish each other's movements.

LILY dips a piece of bread into the sauce, tastes it.

HELEN: We cook what we can't say.

LILY: Yes.

The sauce boils. LILY adds the potato starch, stirs it vigorously.

HELEN dips a piece of bread in the sauce, tastes it.

HELEN: Takes me home… Popo.

LILY: Yes love.

HELEN: I'm always happiest in the kitchen cooking with you. Becoming a lawyer was never my dream. It was yours.

LILY looks at HELEN, pours the ingredients into a clay pot, turns the heat down.

The light shifts with the movement of the boat.

LILY: On this boat… As I cook I start to dream again.

HELEN: I have a good job, earn good money.

LILY: I remember this… Is this ambition?

HELEN: But it's not enough.

LILY: Hope?

HELEN: It's not my passion.

LILY: I'll save. I'll send money home. I'll save.

HELEN: I have saved but for what?

LILY: One day… I'll live with Mabel again.

HELEN reaches for a pak choi, tears off leaves and adds them to the pot.

LILY: Everything?

HELEN: Yes.

HELEN stirs the ingredients. The smell fills the theatre.

LILY: I want to be my own boss.

HELEN: Me too.

The light shifts with the movement of the boat.

A table appears. LEUNG enters carrying a fish on a platter.

LILY: We ate Salmon with soy at my twelfth birthday banquet.

LEUNG: Save the eyes for Lily.

LEUNG sets the fish down on the table.

HELEN: Urgh…

LEUNG lights a stick of incense and places it in a plant pot, takes his place at the table.

LILY: I'm Leung's daughter.

HELEN: I'm his great granddaughter.

TAI PO enters carrying a golden birds nest stuffed with vegetables. She sets the dish down, lights incense and takes her place at the table.

LILY: With time I'm myself again.

LILY carries MABEL's claypot chicken to the table, sets it down.

HELEN: I'm whole.

MABEL enters carrying a dish, sets it down. She looks at HELEN, goes over and gives her a hug. MABEL lights a stick of incense and takes her place at the table.

HELEN: I know who I am now. Know what I want. The recipes…

LILY lights a stick of incense and takes her place at the table.

LILY: We'll always have them, pass them down.

HELEN carries the rice to the table, looks at the family dishes.

HELEN: The recipes are my future.

HELEN lights a stick of incense, looks around the table, two empty spaces. HELEN sits down in one of the spaces.

Both HELEN and LILY look at the one empty space.

LILY serves MABEL rice and then the claypot chicken.

HELEN & LILY: *(English & Cantonese.)* If the mountains are level… We're free.

HELEN serves the food and the family starts to eat.

Lights down.

By the same author

P'yongyang
9781783193332

This Isn't Romance
9781840029109

WWW.OBERONBOOKS.COM

Follow us on www.twitter.com/@oberonbooks
& www.facebook.com/OberonBooksLondon